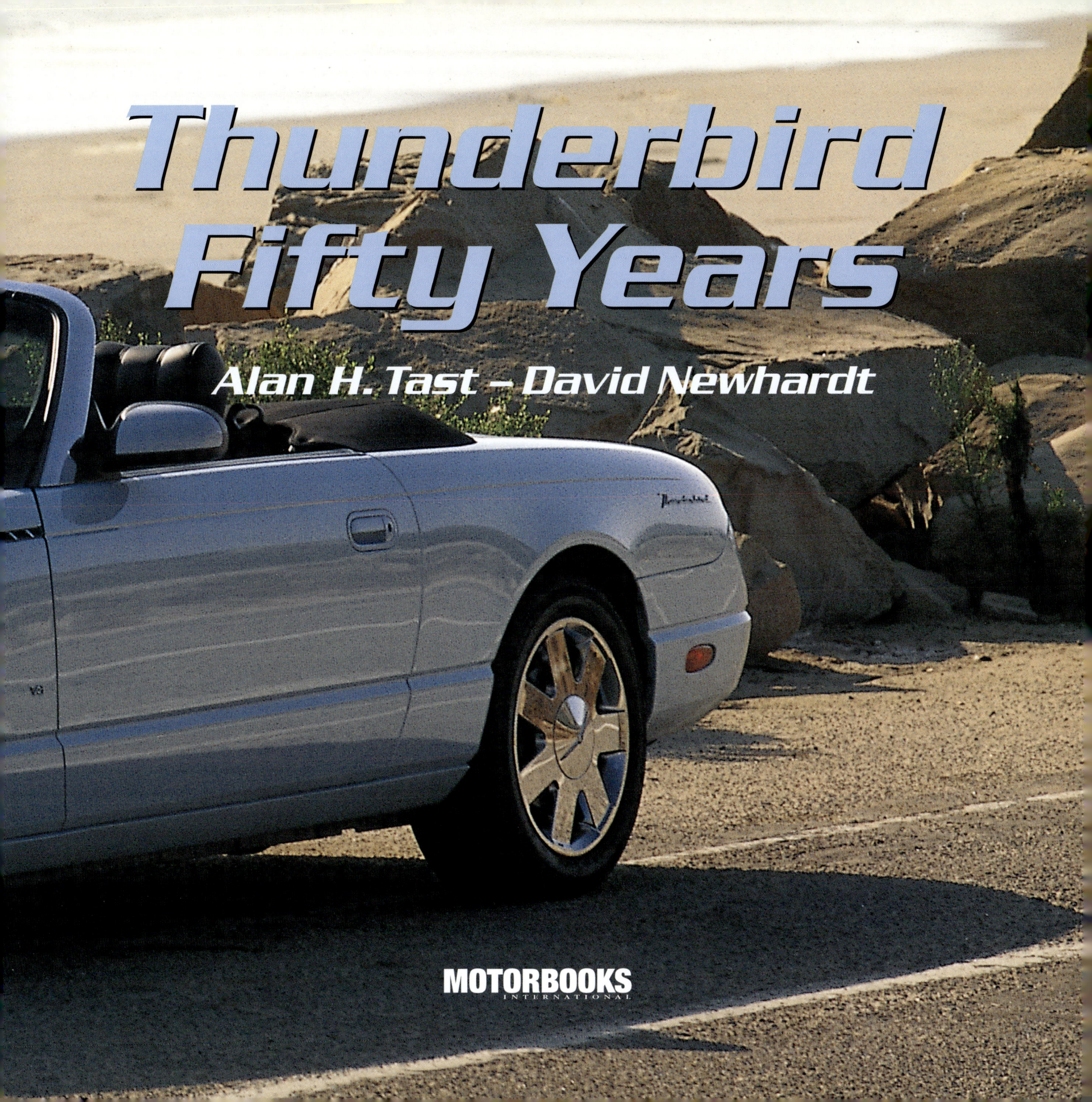

Thunderbird Fifty Years

Alan H. Tast – David Newhardt

MOTORBOOKS INTERNATIONAL

First published in 2004 by Motorbooks International, an imprint of MBI Publishing Company, Galtier Plaza, Suite 200, 380 Jackson Street, St. Paul, MN 55101-3885 USA

© Alan H. Tast and David Newhardt, 2004

All rights reserved. With the exception of quoting brief passages for the purposes of review, no part of this publication may be reproduced without prior written permission from the Publisher.

The information in this book is true and complete to the best of our knowledge. All recommendations are made without any guarantee on the part of the author or Publisher, who also disclaim any liability incurred in connection with the use of this data or specific details.

This publication has not been prepared, approved, or licensed by Ford. We recognize, further, that some words, model names, and designations mentioned herein are the property of the trademark holder. We use them for identification purposes only. This is not an official publication.

Motorbooks International titles are also available at discounts in bulk quantity for industrial or sales-promotional use. For details write to Special Sales Manager at Motorbooks International Wholesalers & Distributors, Galtier Plaza, Suite 200, 380 Jackson Street, St. Paul, MN 55101-3885 USA.

ISBN 0-7603-1976-6

On the cover: Basking in a Southern California sunset is Bill Evans' 1957 Thunderbird and a 2004 Thunderbird from Ford Motor Company's press fleet. The generational similarities are unmistakable.

On the frontispiece: 2003 T-Bird

On the title page 2003 T-Bird

On the back cover: Wire wheels from 1962–1964 Thunderbirds are a popular addition to Little 'Birds. A wire wheel cover was available, but very cumbersome to install.

Edited by: Amy Glaser
Designed by: Kari Johnston

Printed in China

Contents

Introduction 6

Chapter 1	1955–1957	Instant Classic 12
Chapter 2	1958–1960	Four Square 36
Chapter 3	1961–1963	Speeding Bullet 50
Chapter 4	1964–1966	Rolling Sculpture 66
Chapter 5	1967–1969	Mature for Its Age 82
Chapter 6	1970–1971	The Beak Goes On 96
Chapter 7	1972–1976	Luxury Land Yacht 104
Chapter 8	1977–1979	Trim & Proper 116
Chapter 9	1980–1982	Retrenchment—Wrong Place, Wrong Time 126
Chapter 10	1983–1986	Aero Coup 134
Chapter 11	1987–1988	Raw, but Refined 146
Chapter 12	1989–1997	Super 154
Chapter 13	2002–2005	Resurrection 172

Appendix 188

Index 191

Thunderbird Fifty Years

Introduction

(above and opposite) 1955 T-Bird

(opposite) Aside from Chevrolet's Corvette, others attempted to capitalize on two-seat sports cars, such as the Dutch Darrin-designed offering from Kaiser-Frazier. John Lee

This is the first Corvette, circa 1953. Alan H. Tast collection

At the beginning of the second half of the twentieth century, civilization was at a crossroads. In just 50 years, people had gone from riding horses to flying supersonic airplanes. The average person, who at the beginning of the century relied on the agrarian economy and muscular labor for a living, was now living in a city or suburb and punching a time clock. Local tastes in news and entertainment became worldwide with the development of radio and, more recently, the magic box known as television. Nations had gone through the horrors of two world wars, a devastating economical depression, and now were riding a wave of technological prosperity. People were living better, had more money to spend, and were looking to the future as something to embrace.

People had more disposable income than ever before, and more choices than ever for spending it. Those who had spent the years after World War II in college on the GI Bill were now becoming upwardly mobile professionals, and dreams once deferred were now coming to fruition. A new single-family house with all the comforts of modern living meant stability. However, a flashy new automobile in the driveway was a status symbol that let neighbors know the owner had "made it," or was on the rise.

There was a shortage of status symbols in the early 1950s. The nation was more concerned with Communism, and looked for a

Jaguar's XK-120 had a major influence on Ford's pending sports car program. Alan H. Tast collection

10 *Introduction*

post-war identity. New leaders were coming forward, and the optimism of a generation rested on their shoulders. Such was the case at Ford Motor Company. Founder Henry Ford passed away on April 7, 1947, and with him went his conservative views on how the company should approach the growing automobile marketplace. Grandson Henry Ford II was well on his way to revamping how the company did business, and responding to what people wanted. The people wanted something new, exciting, and stylish.

In the period just after World War II, people had to live with whatever car manufacturers churned out, which was a rehash of the vehicles they produced before retooling their factories to serve the war effort. Designing and fabricating a new line of cars took years to accomplish The cars coming out of Detroit by 1950 were finally breaking away from running boards and pontoon fenders, but there was still something lacking—something that would take a person's breath away.

There were sporting cars on American roads following the war. They did not come from our factories, but from soldiers who returned with them from across the Atlantic—sports cars by Jaguar, Triumph, MG, and others. Smaller, nimbler, with wind-in-the-face excitement, they promised a novelty at the wheel that larger, more ponderous American cars did not deliver. Yet, not every U.S. driver liked the raw, unrefined openness of a true sports car. That's where good, old American ingenuity, and Ford Motor Company, were ready to step in.

Ford's first shot at a personal luxury sports model was a bull's eye—the start of a 50-year run as one of the world's most widely recognized automobiles. From repeat "Car of the Year" awards to repeat NASCAR victories, the Thunderbird proved its mettle again and again on the road, track, and drafting table. Most important, it proved itself in the hearts of millions of fans around the globe. Even when the century ran out, and with it Ford's use for the Thunderbird, the car's charm carried it forward. Working without a budget, without compensation—and without permission—designers took it upon themselves to rescue an icon. Their vision and commitment saved the day, and gave the T-Bird new life in a style capturing the essence of that first, postwar sensation.

For 50 years aloft, here's to the Ford Thunderbird...

CHAPTER ONE

1955–1957
Instant Classic

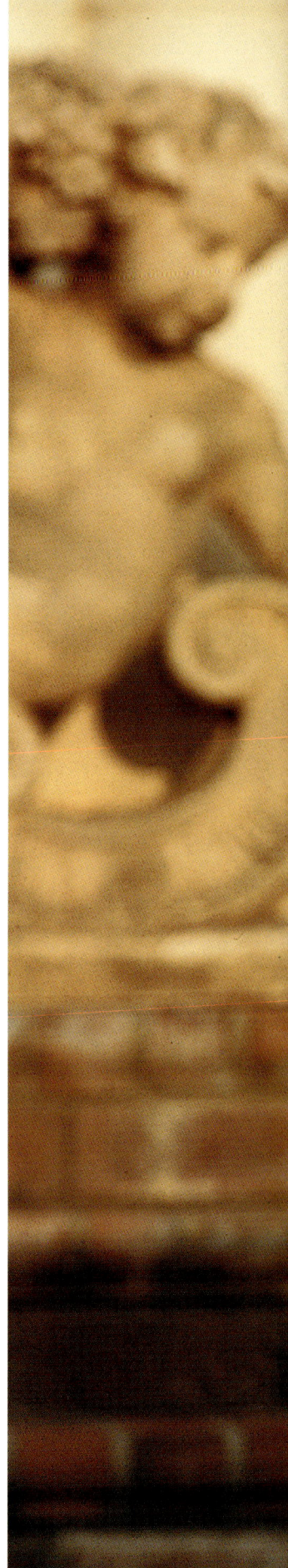

The taillights were shared with the 1955 full-size Ford to reduce costs and create a cross-model tie-in.

(opposite) When George Watts began to research the history of "005," he learned that it was used in a 1954 Sports Illustrated road test and fitted with 1955 Fairlane eyebrow headlight doors.

By the beginning of the 1950s, Ford was searching for new style. Pre-war designs were out of date, and the passing of Henry Ford in 1947 freed the company from his conservative influence. Under Henry Ford II, the company made some strategic hires in its quest to put a new face on the Ford lineup. One of the new hires was veteran designer Frank Hershey. Hershey learned his craft from the ground up by sketching and working out details on custom-built cars in California before joining the General Motors design staff in the 1930s. There, under Harley Earl, he helped develop such trademarks as the Pontiac Silver Streak and the finned taillight housings on the 1949 Cadillac. He joined Ford just as the design staff was starting work to update the 1954 Ford and develop the 1955 models. Hershey and his assistants started playing with ways to make the new generation look lower, longer, and sleeker than anything previous. They wanted to build something sportier than a family sedan.

In the basements and back rooms of Ford's engineering buildings, a very small group of engineers and designers were given a chance to lay out what they thought a Ford sports car should be. By the spring of 1952, Hershey and his team knew that their competitor, General Motors was already well on its way to producing an American version of the two-seat, close-coupled sports cars that were imported from jolly old England. They knew that it would be made of fiberglass, a new material that could be molded into virtually any shape. They also knew that GM aimed to spring this on the public within the coming year.

Ford designers felt the squeeze. They had to have an answer to the impending Corvette, but it couldn't bear the trappings of a rush job. The design had to win public acceptance—and before that, it had to win upper management's approval. During the course of 1952, the new Ford sports car dominated the spare time of Hershey and his team. Sketches littered drawing tables, full-size body renderings stood against walls, and large chalkboards offered designers ready workspace to evaluate possibilities. Meanwhile, planners pored over market data to determine how to package the car.

And then, the dam broke.

In January 1953, New York's Waldorf Astoria hotel played host to General Motors' display of new ideas called "Motorama." Taking center stage was a small, white car with rounded lines, wire mesh over the headlights, and an open cockpit with individual bucket seats. Named Corvette after a small, fast type of warship, it took America by surprise. Not only was it a dream car, it was being readied for immediate production. Ford executives who were not in the loop about what was going on were in a panic—how quickly could they have a response to this? Little did they know, their own people were well on the way with a rebuttal. Within two months, full-size mock-ups of the new Ford were made available for Henry and other decision-makers to look at and feel. With suggestions coming out of these viewings, the sporty Ford was on the way for a date with destiny.

One year after the Corvette's unveiling, Ford's retort was ready for its coming-out party. The intervening months gave designers, engineers, and others a chance to study the two-seat Chevrolet's shortcomings and gauge public reaction. It was underpowered,

(opposite) This black 1955 (serial number P5FH10005) is considered the "first" production Thunderbird. It was originally restored by George Watts in 1965 and has been maintained as a true historic treasure.

(above) In 1955, the exhaust pipes went through the body in chromed housings, but the pipes went through the bumper ends in 1956 and 1957.

(right) Wire wheels from 1962–1964 Thunderbirds are a popular addition to Little 'Birds. A wire wheel cover was available, but very cumbersome to install.

uncomfortable, and too bizarre-looking. No roll-up windows and other conveniences that people were taking for granted in their sedans made it even more of a target for betterment. Ford's car could easily address the Corvette's shortcomings.

On February 20, 1954, Ford introduced the result of its two-year effort at the Detroit Auto Show. It was named "Thunderbird" by stylist Alden Giberson, who submitted the name in a contest with others involved with the project. The car almost didn't get its storied moniker. A few days before the show, the project team learned that the company's attorneys hadn't filed the trademark application. In a mad rush to register the name, they narrowly beat competitor GM, which had planned to use the same title for an experimental concept car. Beaten to the punch, GM had to settle on its second choice, Firebird. Emblazoned with scripts for its new title and the Fairlane line of new Fords, with which it shared its characteristic looks—including side chrome trim deleted before production—the turquoise-painted Thunderbird became the most talked-about model in town.

Enthusiast publications heralded the news that Ford now had a steel-bodied sports car to match the fiberglass Corvette, but the publicists were quick to point out that the Thunderbird was not a sports car in the same fashion that the Chevrolet, MG, and Jag-types were accustomed. On the contrary, it was a "personal luxury" car with power-assisted windows, steering, brakes, and a four-way seat; it also offered a heater, radio, and choice of three-speed, overdrive, or automatic transmissions. Plus with Ford's all-new Y-block sitting between the inner fenders, it would have enough go-power to cruise effortlessly down the new interstates that were being constructed at President Eisenhower's behest.

Potential buyers were taunted by the car's reverse-wedge design, hints of elongated dorsal fins, and motion-evoking headlight bezels. The stamped, stainless-steel mesh grille was an interpretation of the egg-crate grilles on the Ferrari race cars eating up European road courses. A "power dome" rose up from the center of the hood to clear the air cleaner. Its chrome-plated, grilled opening allowed air to enter and force itself into the four-barrel carburetor, while chrome-plated, forward-canted emblems looked like exhaust louvers. To take full advantage of interior space, the show car employed a

This is a rare view of the Thunderbird prototype show car taken prior to its introduction at the 1954 Detroit Auto Show. It illustrates several interesting differences from the production version, including the high-hat air cleaner on a 1954 Mercury engine, quilted hood liner, parallel hood hinges, deep-pile carpeting, and chrome shifter knob.
Courtesy John Smith

Shortly before it was released for production, Ford toyed with the idea of installing Fairlane-style trim. Ford Motor Company, Alan H. Tast collection

bench seat with bucket-like inserts. It could hold three people in a pinch, but it really was better suited for two. The design was futuristic, yet it shared styling cues with the rest of the Ford lineup.

After a series of pre-production refinements—including Hershey's victory in removing the full-size Fairlane's "check-mark" side trim against the wishes of new vice president of styling George Walker—the car was ready for production. On September 9, 1954, the first production cars rolled through the final inspection and acceptance area of the Dearborn Assembly Plant along the River Rouge. They were expedited into the hands of automotive critics and other people of influence. Within two months Ford had manufactured enough Thunderbirds to allow distribution throughout the company's empire. On October 22, the car was unveiled in dealerships across the United States for exhibition. A reported 4,000 people left deposits that day to secure the new sensation—prompting the company to radically revise sales estimates upward from the initial projection of 10,000 cars.

The Thunderbird was well-proportioned. Its overall length of 175.3 inches was almost 2 feet shorter than the 198.2 inches of the full-size Ford, but only 2.1 inches narrower and 8.8 inches shorter when the hardtop was installed. Its overall length and 102-inch wheelbase—a full 13.5 inches shorter than the sedans—coupled with a 56-inch front tread width (2 inches narrower than the full-size mother ship) meant that a unique frame had to be used to carry the unit constructed body. The rear track width of 56 inches was the same as the full-size car. Ford contracted with the Budd Corporation to assemble the bodies, finish the metal, and truck to the Rouge unpainted shells, which were then inserted into the plant-built full-size cars. The 23-to-1 steering ratio was much less responsive than that used in true sports cars, and steering and frame geometry yielded a fairly large turning radius of 36 feet. With 11-inch diameter drums on all four corners and 175 square-inches of lining area, the brakes did not score high with drivers, who complained of fade during successive hard stops.

Exterior ornamentation was simple. Stainless-steel trim surrounded the grille opening, and chrome-plated bumpers protected the forward and rear extremities. A pair of housings bolted to the bumper acted as guards for the front, and they could be fitted with optional driving lights. Originally fitted further outboard, they restricted the flow of air into the ducts that fed the interior; for production, the housings were moved closer to the center. Because of the low 5.5-inch ground clearance, the exhaust pipes were routed through the body and out the back through a similar set of housings. The surrounds for the exhaust outlets through the housings would change design from a "doughnut" style to a tri-bar pattern in mid-production to mimic the front bumper housing inserts.

(above) Sunset Coral was added in March 1956 and represents one of three spring colors. The others were Goldenglow Yellow and Navajo Gray.

(left) Back-up light housings and turn signal lenses changed in 1956 and used full-size Ford assemblies.

The Ford's new crowned crest adorned the nose panel and gas door, along with a pair of crossed, checkered flags; only the crest was used on the side of the hardtop. In front of the "hash marks," a pair of red background emblems with an "8" juxtaposed over a "Y" (for Y-block) advertised that the car had a V-8 engine. Ford offered three basic colors initially, Raven Black, Torch Red and Thunderbird Blue. The company added Snowshoe White after the beginning of the year, and Goldenrod Yellow in March.

The V-8 running gear was Ford-derived—a 292-ci variant of the Mercury engine that was built in Cleveland, Ohio, and shipped to Dearborn for installation. It used a Holley 4000 four-venturi downdraft carburetor and produced 193 horsepower at 4,400 rpm with 280 foot-pounds of torque at 2,500 rpm, when joined with a manual gearbox. To overcome the drag imposed by all the parts of the three-speed Ford-O-Matic (low gear was a manual selection, second and third were automatic from the "D" position), a bump in compression from 8.1 to 8.5:1 increased output to 198 ponies and 285 foot-pounds at the same revs. The engine was mounted rearward and nearly buried into the firewall in order to allow room for the radiator and water pump-mounted cooling fan, as well as to move the center of gravity toward the center of the car for a 52/48 weight ratio over the wheels. Its performance against a 265-ci V-8 Corvette was marginally better at the upper end, but

Before the porthole hardtop came along, a more-conventional B-pillar window was considered.
Courtesy Tim Roden

Part of the inspiration for the rear-mounted spare came from the first generation of the Lincoln Continental. Alan H. Tast

from the hole, it was outgunned in part because of the Thunderbird's curb weight of 3,382 pounds versus the Corvette's 2,810. Once the larger 292 started flowing the torque to the 3.31:1 rear axle in an automatic-equipped car, the T-Bird gained the advantage.

A big part of the Thunderbird's appeal was its engine with a dress-up kit installed. While the use of brightwork on the exterior was tastefully restrained, under the hood there was a lot of it. The carburetor was shrouded by a chrome-plated dome of sheet metal. Valve covers, held in place with two chrome-plated acorn nuts, were provided in

Before Ford offered a supercharger, McCullough/Paxton offered kits for installation, such as this one on a 1955 T-Bird. Alan H. Tast

The Battlebirds used two engines—one with the Lincoln 430, and the other (shown here) with a modified 312-ci engine equipped with Hilborn injectors. The engine was moved back into the firewall to improve handling. Alan H. Tast

cast aluminum with narrow fins that sported a raised and painted Thunderbird emblem. Various components like the oil filler cap and even the three-bladed cooling fan were given the shiny treatment. Over time, the three-blade fan failed as hydrogen embrittlement took its toll, but the other parts would be used through the next two years. Cars not fitted with the dress-up kit used black-painted valve covers with decals to denote the engine type and a silver-painted air cleaner.

Interior details were not lacking. A vinyl-covered and texture-painted dashboard softened its feel, while engine-turned aluminum panels brightened up the surroundings. Instrumentation used the full-size Ford's novel Astra-Dial speedometer, flanked by a clock and mechanical tachometer driven by the distributor. Ribbed vinyl-covered door panels featured padded armrests that swooped down from the lower edge of the dash. Wall-to-wall carpeting with jute padding insulated the lower extremities from the floor pan, but the position of the engine, transmission, dual exhaust pipe routing, and mufflers under the seat area still created an overheated interior. In the spring of 1955, Ford expanded the original interior color choices—red/white, black/white, and aqua/white—with a black and yellow "bumblebee" mix. The 14.0-cubic-foot trunk was more simple, with a rubber mat lining the floor; the 15-inch spare wheel with 6.70x15 tire reduced its usable volume to 11.6 cubic feet.

Ford offered two ways to enclose the cockpit. Buyers could choose a convertible top that could be stowed behind the seat under a drop curtain, a removable fiberglass hardtop, or both. The convertible top had a swing-arm arrangement that was difficult to get into place quickly—a drawback in a sudden rainstorm. Its folding action was somewhat weak and it didn't do a good job of sealing out the weather. The hardtop had its problems, too. The large side area behind the driver created a blind spot that made it difficult to see traffic to the side and rear of the car, and it rubbed on the rear deck's paint, creating unsightly lines when the top was removed. Several items were changed and upgraded on both tops through the course of production, including drip rails for the hardtop and header bow trim for the soft top.

Flaws notwithstanding, the $2,944 initial price tag was not a stumbling block in comparison to the $2,324 for a full-size Sunliner. When production ended at 16,155 units in September 1955, it vastly outsold Corvette's 700-unit output and nearly sealed its fate—had Chevrolet not upgraded it with its new small-block V-8 engine. Ford's leadership couldn't be happier with the outpouring of affection for their new personal car, except for one person: Robert S. McNamara. McNamara was pragmatic and earned his keep as a person who looked for ways to keep his employer financially secure and growing. He was the person in line to take over as vice president and general manager of Ford Division from Lewis Crusoe, who was being groomed to step into the shoes of corporate president Ernest Breech at the beginning of 1955. Crusoe saw the Thunderbird as a "halo" car that generated good press and public response toward the entire lineup of family sedans, station wagons, and pickup trucks. Crusoe never saw the car as a high-volume offering, and

Thunderbird's trademark chrome air cleaner was needed to clear the tall four-barrel carburetor. The hood was domed to clear the air cleaner.

(right) "Where were you in '62?" The movie American Graffiti *featured this 1956 and solidified the porthole hardtop's status as a cultural icon.*

(opposite) Thirty-two years after it appeared in American Graffiti, *the vehicle Suzanne Sommers drove in the movie looks as if it is still ready for the next take. Eyebrow headlight trim from a 1955 Fairlane and narrow whitewalls are deviations from the original.*

recognized it as a "loss leader"—in that it would not be able to be sold for what it cost to develop and build. This meant that Ford took a loss on every T-Bird it sold, but the Birds also brought people into the showrooms to buy Customlines and Fairlanes, instead of going across the street to buy Belvederes and Bel-Airs.

McNamara didn't see things this way. Instead, any project put forward had to carry its own weight. If it didn't, it was gone. Although things move slowly in a large manufacturing company, it was tough to counteract what already was in place. McNamara's gut reaction to the two-seat Ford was that if it couldn't be made profitable, it would be forced into early retirement. Since 1956 models were already being readied for final production

acceptance and the 1957s were in advanced stages of engineering prototype work, he would be saddled with the car for at least two more model years.

Crusoe and Henry II were definitely in love with the car; so much, in fact, that their suggestions on how to improve it yielded two characteristics that turned the car into an icon: the porthole top and the rear-mounted spare wheel. After its introduction in the fall of 1954, both men were provided with new Thunderbirds to tool around in and to get their reactions for improvements to implement on the 1956 model. Henry's primary complaint was that the trunk wasn't large enough to carry a set of golf clubs without taking out the spare tire. Crusoe lamented that the hardtop's blank side slab was a driving hazard. He had already nearly been hit while making a "Michigan Left" onto Woodward Avenue. Engineers and stylists were immediately called in to address these issues.

The 1962–1964-style wire wheels for Little 'Birds were so popular that reproductions with the correct 15x5-inch rim are available to use with original-style wide whitewall tires.

To resolve the tire stowage/trunk room issue, the trunk would have to be lengthened for a tire well, but it was too late for 1956 tooling. So, a compromise was developed: mount the spare wheel on a hinged bracket outside of the trunk, and wrap a heavy, chrome-plated bumper extension around it. The result couldn't have been timed better. A new Lincoln luxury coupe, the Continental Mark II, would also come out with a hump in the deck lid to conceal its spare tire. The "Continental Kit" was born.

For the hardtop, designers conducted several studies to remove the blind spot. Early prototypes used a hardtop similar to the Corvette, with a framed piece of glass between the door window and the rear edge of the roof. Not only did this look like Ford was plagiarizing the 'Vette, it was also problematic to remove and store since the glass and frame were easily knocked out of position and broken. The solution was as simple as cutting a circular hole in the side of the top and adding a chrome-framed tempered glass window. The porthole top would become the most popular offering on all the 1956 and 1957 models.

Aside from the top and the rear bumper, styling changes were relatively minor and primarily focused on trim work. The winged emblem used on the dashboard was adapted for use on the front nose with a plastic insert. Tail and backup lights were changed to use the same ones as the full-size 1956 Ford. To cure hot-foot complaints, cowl vents were cut into the fenders and a set of operable doors was installed to regulate airflow into the passenger compartment. The seat and door patterns were slightly modified to add distinction from the 1955 models. In addition, color selections were expanded for the exterior. In March of 1956, Goldenglow Yellow and Sunset Coral were added to the original seven standard colors listed for the exterior, while Navajo Gray replaced the original Thunderbird Gray. Interior colors expanded to six choices, while soft tops were still limited to black or white. The steering wheel became a three-spoke dished affair to tie in with Ford's "Lifeguard Design" program to increase passenger safety. Marketing such things as seatbelts, a padded dash cover, and sun visors, Ford hoped to capitalize on an increasing public awareness of vehicle accidents and injuries resulting from impact with interior components and glass. As Ford would soon learn, it would be more power that would actually increase sales.

To increase the distance in the horsepower race between it and Chevrolet, Ford released an even-larger Y-block—the 312-ci engine. With unique ratings for manual/automatic transmissions of 215/225 horsepower at 4,600 rpm and 317/324 foot-pounds of torque using an 8.4:1 compression ratio, the 312 was Ford's hot engine with the Holley 4000-series four-barrel, which now featured an automatic choke attached directly to the carburetor instead o fon the side ofthe intake manifold. The standard M-code 292 also got a power boost.

Debuted on November 30, 1955, Thunderbird took another run at pumping up Ford's public image and capturing the imagination of wannabe owners around the world. With the major flaws band-aided for the year, the product teams could move on to getting the

Prepared for all-out competition, the Battlebirds were stripped of unnecessary weight. The dash was replaced with a layout of gauges and switches. Alan H. Tast

(above) One of the D/F cars originally built for competition in early 1957 was this Flame Red example.

(right) For many years, enthusiasts thought only 14 D-coded 1957s were built with a Phase I supercharger. The discovery of an invoice for a 15th D/F car in the early 2000s has added to the number.

next version ready for 1957. Though it wasn't much of a competitor for the T-Bird in sales, the Corvette was reinvented and came out looking much more contemporary. Chevy enhanced its performance with dual four-barrel carburetors, and once again Ford was compelled to respond. A dealer-available two-four setup was developed for the Bird, as well as the full-size Ford, for use in competitive venues such as at Daytona Speed Week, which set the tone for the year's sporting events. Dual quads would become a factory option at the beginning of the next model year.

The 15 D/F cars were equipped with virtually no options so they weren't hampered by speed-robbing weight. One of the few options was Safety Package A.

Thunderbird came through the end of the model year with fewer sales, in part because of the shorter period production run and an increase in price to $3,151 for a stripped-down version. Options for the car could send its price well over $4,000. It also gained 108 pounds, much of it due to the outside-mounted spare's hardware. A total of 15,631 were built and sold—a slight decline, but still much better than Corvette's numbers.

On October 1, 1956, dealers were allowed to show their customers the new 1957 Ford line. Completely new from the ground up, they would vie with a restyled Chevrolet for sales supremacy throughout the coming months. Alongside the new Fairlane 500s and lesser models was a new manifestation of the Thunderbird, dolled up to look more like other 1957 Fords, yet retaining the past two years' overall appearance. McNamara's clampdown on expenditures for the two-seater put the kibosh on a complete restyle for both the front and rear ends, leaving enough funding to bring the rear more in line with the full-size car, with canted fins and the full-size Ford's turn signal housing/lens combination. This funding also allowed body engineers to insert the well needed to return the spare tire to the trunk without it consuming so much luggage space and lengthen the body by 6.1 inches. Designers revised the front bumper shape, in part to hide the holes where parking lights appeared two years running. They placed a new nameplate forward of the chrome hash marks. Changing to 14-inch wheels and 7.50x15 tires gave the car a lower-riding stance and dropped the overall height by over half an inch with the hardtop in place. The changes gave the car six more inches in length in the trunk area, for an overall measurement of 182.0 inches, with a width of 72.8 inches across the fins. New colors gave buyers a choice of ten stock hues with the option to special-order other Ford product tints. Customers could even special-order the car with a color of their own choosing, or have it delivered in primer

The Starmist Blue exterior color was offered through August 1957.

The look of a 1957 'Bird with the top down, long rear deck, canted fins, and fender skirts evokes an image of speed and grace.

for their own treatment. Hardtops could be body color or a contrasting one, and soft tops now came in four colors—black, white, blue, and tan.

The interior got a new dashboard that was a mix of the early car's sheet metal with the hooded instrument panel of the 1956 full-size Ford (originally designed for use in the 1955 Thunderbird). Upholstery also got a new look with embossed door panels featuring Thunderbird silhouettes, and horizontal pleats on the seat inserts. Six upholstery colors were available, including two tones of blue, two tones of green, black and white combined, solid red, solid bronze and all white with black carpeting.

The power plants captivated peoples' attention more than the restyling. The same 292- and 312-ci blocks were again available, but in four different versions, and with hiked-up compression ratios. The budget-minded buyer could get an entry-level car with virtually no options for $3,408. This car featured a C-code 292-ci two-barrel carbed engine rated at 212 horsepower at 4,500 rpm and 297 foot-pounds of torque at 2,300 rpm with a three-speed manual transmission. Less-frugal types could opt for two kinds of Thunderbird Special V-8s: the D-code version using a low-profile Holley 4150 four-barrel, or the two-foured "E" setup using a modified Holley 4000s from the 1956 Lincoln.

The D-engined car, capable of producing 245 horses at 4,500 rpm and 332 foot-pounds of torque at 2,300 rpm, was by far the most popular, especially when teamed with the floor-shifted Ford-O-Matic (it could also be had with the overdrive manual transmission). On the semi-wild side, the street-tuned "E" raised the bar by 30 ponies at 300 additional turns per minute over the "D," and pegged the torque-meter at 336 foot-

pounds at a faster 3,400 rpm. Bonafide race car drivers in the know could get an upgrade for the "E" with stiffer valve springs, a different cam, 10.0:1 compression, and other tweaks to up the ante to 285 whinnies with the crank whirling at 5,000 rpm.

Yet, the most impressive and hard-to-get engine was the supercharged F-code 312. Using a belt-driven McCullough/Paxton VR57 centrifugal air pump hung off the front of the engine, the "F" was intended to be an all-out racing package. Ford first prepared 15 such cars for race teams in California, North Carolina, and Florida, starting with D-code cars with virtually no options. The Holley low-profile four-barrel was replaced with a modified Lincoln version of the high-rise Holley that accommodated the higher airflow rate produced by the blower. The two were connected with a combination of a cast-aluminum bonnet over the throat of the carburetor and a large-diameter rubber hose. To handle the 6 pounds of boost, compression was dropped to 8.5:1. Dyno tests showed a tire-shredding 340 horses at 5,300 rpm. In a variety of speed contests on the beach and road race courses around Daytona during the beginning of February 1957, the blown cars outperformed similarly equipped Studebaker Golden Hawks, fuel-injected Corvettes, and just about everything else that could be thrown at them.

By this time, more than race fans and gearheads were taking notice of manufacturers' all-out efforts to promote their products with high performance. Congress began holding hearings to investigate how the growth of more powerful and faster cars was endangering the motoring public. To head off potential federal regulations, the Automotive Manufacturers Association decided in May to request that companies get out of racing.

Four is good, but eight is better. The optional E-series for 1957 featured two raised domes to fit over the two Holley 4000s. The filter chamber on versions through December 1956 were oval. The later ones, such as the one shown, were round.

A plethora of body and hardtop color combinations were available for 1957, such as Coral Sand and Raven Black, as shown here.

(above) Azure Blue is a color that was available from September 1957 through the end of production.

(above left) Headlight doors for 1957 were shared with lower-level 1956 Fords. Plans to restyle the front fenders and headlights to match the 1957 Ford were put on hold to keep costs down.

(left) Turbine-style wheel covers, stainless steel–trimmed fender skirts, and wide whitewall tires were popular options for 1957.

McNamara was among the first to be a good corporate citizen to sign the ban, which also gave him a reason to stop spending money on what he considered to be a trivial pursuit. At the same time, McCullough, Paxton, and Ford engineers were developing a revised VR-57A blower for full-size Fords and T-Birds. The new chargers used a beefed up, ribbed housing that bolted together instead of using a band clamp to handle the pressure of sustained driving. The agreement to end racing efforts likewise derailed full-race setups. The remaining street-legal installations were tuned to produce 300 horses at 4,800 rpm. Records conflict as to Phase II F-Birds total production, but at least 194 were invoiced by the end of the model year.

With the 1958 full-size line set for release in late September 1957, Ford management realized they could not get the new Thunderbird ready until after the beginning of the new year. To keep the Thunderbird in public view, the company extended production well beyond the typical August cut-off point. Late-production Birds built from September on still were titled as 1957s, but employed bits and pieces of 1958s as parts stock was depleted for things such as window crank knobs, which changed from black to white. These late-production cars used five exterior colors from the 1958 full-size line, with some colors

Even though the original 430-engined No. 99 Battlebird was wrecked in the early 1960s, a replica of it can be seen at historic races such as Monterey. The second car, No. 98, survived and was restored in the early 1990s.

(above) Using a lower-profile carburetor, single-carbed engines for 1957 used a shorter cover. The cork lip on the front helped direct air into the filter from the hood scoop.

(above right) Cast-aluminum valve covers with the T-Bird emblem were part of the $21.50 Engine Dress-Up Kit.

(right) The T-Bird ornament on the deck lid doubles as a handle.

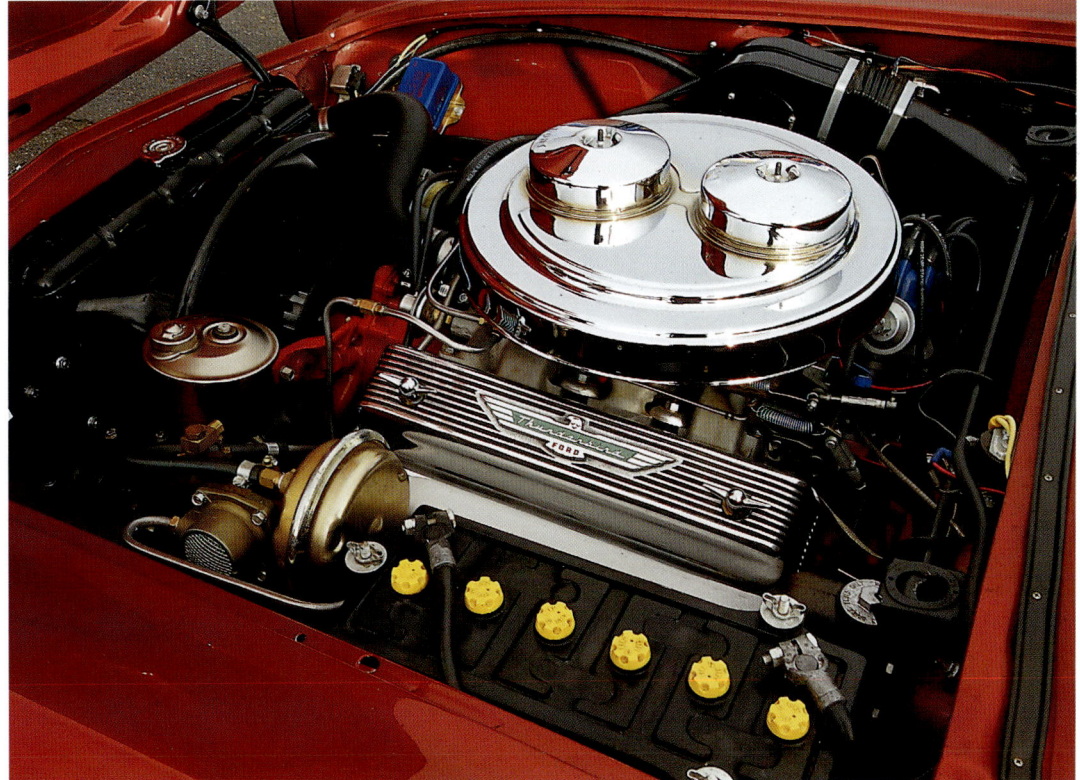

(left) A desirable E-series 1957 model reveals components of the Engine Dress-Up Kit and accessories such as a heater, power steering, and power brakes. Wing nuts on the valve covers are an aftermarket item.

carried over from 1957, to keep things simple for painters. But, the time to wrap it up had to come, and on December 13, 1957, the last of the two-seat Thunderbirds was driven off the line. In the end, 21,380 of the 1957s left Dearborn Assembly to find homes around the world. Most were built-up, ready-to run vehicles, while some were sold in knocked-down, crated-up form for assembly at Ford's LaVilla plant in Mexico City, Mexico, and other foreign locales to get around luxury and import tariffs.

Time would be very kind to the Little Bird. Its brief run created a demand for them well after the full-size Fords had rolled their last mile. Recognizing that they were special cars, many owners went to great lengths to preserve them, treating the pint-size Fords like priceless gems. Enthusiasts estimate that almost half of the 53,000 classic Thunderbirds are still around. It's probably a safe bet that even 50 years from now, that number will not significantly change.

CHAPTER TWO

1958–1960
Four Square

The Cameo Rose and Winterset White two-tone paint job was a $25.80 option on the 1958 hardtop, as were wide whitewall tires ($36), turbine wheel covers ($17.10), and fender skirts ($26.60).

(opposite) For 1958, two pair of headlights were set over a mesh pattern that matched the grille. The center of the lens could hold backup lights for a $9.50 option.

(above) Two-tone paint schemes were popular in 1959, but Indian Turquoise over Colonial White was somewhat unusual. Dummy spotlights and high-mounted peep mirrors are aftermarket add-ons.

(left) Door handles were styled to blend into the tailfins. For 1959, chrome spear tips were placed on the leading edge of windsplits stamped into the lower body.

Fall 1954 was a critical time for the development of the Thunderbird. Orders for 4,000 cars on "T-Day" convinced upper management that their gamble for a two-seat personal luxury car was going to pay off. Yet representatives throughout the country's sales districts heard one question repeatedly: "Can we get it with four seats?" By that time, design work through the 1957 model was too far along for Ford to consider a major rework.

Ford Division head Robert McNamara was skeptical of the two-seater Thunderbird. At the same time, his marketing people were stressing a gap in Ford's lineup between mid- and upper-priced cars—a place GM occupied with its Buick and Oldsmobile lines. McNamara saw a four-seater Thunderbird as addressing both issues and his budget planners said it could be accomplished for $40 million. This was a fraction of the cost of the Edsel project, which he criticized as a drain on the company's resources.

Robert McNamara, vice president of Ford's car and truck division (front), with James O. Wright, vice president and general manager of Ford Division (center), and Charles Beacham, Assistant General Manager (rear) stand with new products for 1958, including the Thunderbird. Alan H. Tast collection

The new Thunderbird development team produced a basic plan for the car. It would remain smaller and squatter than a full-size Ford or Mercury, receive power from a larger-displacement V-8, come in closed and convertible forms, and provide sufficient room for at least four adults. With the basic specifications in hand, a team led by designers William "Bill" Boyer and David Ash set out to make a statement. By the summer of 1955, they had concept sketches and scale models revealing a twin-pontoon theme with a heavily sculpted form. By November of that year, many of its details still needed to be refined, but a basic shape was there. Over the next five months, the designers worked with engineers to refine the design to a point where final modeling and pre-production work could begin. The result would be like no other Ford to date.

The design called for the car to be built without a frame so that the floor could sit as low to the ground as possible. To accomplish this, engineers used the outer edges of the body and the center tunnel for the transmission and driveshaft to provide structural support. Support is especially important for the convertibles, which lack the additional support provided by a fixed roof. As on the Little Bird body, the front fenders and nose were tied together with the cowl and subframe to further stiffen the assembly. To provide more headroom for rear-seat passengers, the typical sloped backlight was abandoned and the back of the roof squared off

Lincolns such as this 1959, shared the same production line at Wixom, Michigan, with Thunderbirds. John Lee

with a near vertical rear window. The roof was so revolutionary that Ford would adopt it for its mid-year 1959 Galaxie line. By the early 1960s, most manufacturers had a form of it on their cars. The net result was a very rigid, rattle-free body that was very roomy.

The 1958 Lincoln was another unibody car under parallel development. Although larger and heavier, its construction techniques were virtually the same, and not by accident. Planners envisioned the Thunderbird and Lincoln being assembled in the same plant, undergoing construction on 325 acres between Novi and Wixom, Michigan. The 2.5-million-square-foot facility, which opened on April 15, 1957, could able to handle both lines, but only if the Thunderbird shells were assembled off-site and trucked in.

Top management handed down final approvals for the unibody Thunderbird by the spring of 1956. The radical curves and surfaces of the highly sculpted body created manufacturing challenges, from forming the compound curved windshield to stamping out items like the massive bumpers and heavily eyebrowed front fenders. Engineers, tool makers, and vendors had approximately 18 months to have everything ready for the start of production in December 1957.

The new FE-series engines, to be used in Fords and Edsels, proved to be a major development for the engine division. The FE was a deep-skirted Y-block setup with an unique intake manifold/upper cylinder head arrangement. Thunderbird would use the full-size Ford's largest offering of 352-ci, rated at 300 horsepower at 4,600 rpm with 381 foot-pounds of torque at 2,800 rpm—almost 50 foot-pounds better than a D-series 1957. Oversquare 4-inch diameter pistons and a stroke of 3.5 inches were matched originally with 10.2:1 compression heads set up for mechanical lifters, but engineers reduced compression to a more manageable 9.6:1 and switched to hydraulic tappets to reduce valvetrain chatter making it more suitable for a fine luxury car. Offered with a full range of transmissions from a lowly non-synchronized three-speed to a new three-speed Cruise-O-Matic slushbox, a wide range of performance capabilities were available.

With an overall length of 205.4 inches, a staggering 6 feet, 5 inches in width, and a roof height of 52.5 inches, the new Thunderbird was almost 2 feet longer and half a foot wider than the Baby Bird. The wheelbase was stretched to 113 inches, and the track width was widened to 60 inches up front and 57 inches at the rear axle. The new Bird rode on 8.00x14 4-ply tires on 14x5½-inch wheels. Steering was geared for a 25-to-1 ratio, providing for a less-than-taut response made even mushier with hydraulic assist. Brakes with 11-inch drums at all four corners utilized 194 square inches of lining area. Initially, the brakes used ceramic and metallic composition linings, but engineers switched to standard asbestos following complaints about excessive noise with the new material.

The four-place Thunderbird was slated to receive the new Ford-Aire suspension, utilizing air bags to supplement coil springs. Implemented on the full-size Fords in the fall of 1957, Ford-Aire suffered from numerous problems. Ford dropped the T-Bird-adapted system at the last minute and went to conventional coil springs front and rear. A set of stamped steel trailing arms, heavy steel bar links, and a panhard rod were used to hold the Ford 9-inch axle assembly in place. For the 1958 T-Birds, the company abandoned the elliptical rear leafs that had been used on Fords since the 1949 shoebox. However, drive tests and owners squawking about excessive body roll and lean when taking corners at speed brought back leaf springs for 1959 and beyond.

The taller driveshaft tunnel required by the unibody design presented a styling challenge in the interior. Rather than leave it a carpeted mound, the designers instead chose to bisect the car with a full-length, vinyl-coated floor console straddling the hump. This provided a new place to mount power window switches and a radio speaker. The dash was formed into two coves with a foam-padded dash cover that surrounded the instrument cluster and glove box—both handsome plated-metal castings with argent-painted recesses. Between the eyebrows, the radio control head was mounted; above it the optional in-dash air conditioning register was placed, and below in the console's kick-up would be the heater and A/C controls. Front passengers sat in bucket seats. A matching insert theme and padded bolsters gave rear seat occupants a bucket seat type of feel. Doors and quarter panels had padded

Allegheny-Ludlum Steel had two 1960 hardtops constructed with brushed stainless-steel wire-wheel covers were added in the mid-1960s. Alan H. Tast

42   Chapter Two

(above) This Brandywine Red 1959 model is a stunning example of the T-Bird convertible. The narrow whitewalls aren't original.

(opposite) Horizontal ribs in the taillight panel reflect the grille treatment.

armrests in a color that contrasted with the embossed, white door-panel vinyl. A total of four cloth and vinyl, and six two-tone vinyl, combinations were available, as were seven combinations of the four convertible top colors with four basket-weave cloth linings.

Exterior ornamentation was low-key so that it wouldn't clash with the body's contours. The nameplate used for 1957 was placed behind the headlight door casting, five sets of simulated air extractors were placed on the door "bomb," and gunsights from the full-size Ford appeared on the front fender tops. A round emblem, almost identical to the 1957 non-porthole top version, was installed on the C-pillar, above the beltline washboards and behind the intersection of the roof and rear quarter window. A new "Vee-bird" emblem was bolted to the nose panel and rear deck lid. A pattern of circles and lines lifted from the 1958 full-size Ford provided texture for both the front grille and taillight panels, which were deeply recessed into the body. Four large, round lenses were backlit when brakes or turn signals were applied. Twelve exterior color choices at the beginning of the model year were supplemented with at least four other Lincoln or Ford car colors by special order. In August, Ford added Peach and changed from Winterset to Colonial White. Two-tones were available in over three dozen combinations.

Part of Ford's plan to make money on new cars was to offer a host of accessories that people could have installed by dealers or special-order if they chose to fill out the paperwork. Items like an exterior Sports Spare Wheel Carrier, spotlights with mirrors, fender shields that reduced the rear wheel's exposure, power brakes, power steering, and power driver's seat were popular. The base price of $3,630 for a hardtop could escalate rather quickly if the car was fully loaded. Most cars sold for more, with buyers adding power assists and automatic transmissions. Cruise-O-Matics were installed in 98 percent of all Thunderbirds built, leaving standard-shift and overdrive-equipped cars to split the difference. Air conditioning went into 20 percent of all 1958s, and by 1960 this figure would increase to 25 percent. On the opposite end of the spectrum, only two percent of buyers opted not to install a heater or A/C. Power windows found their way into over half of all Squarebirds built, with power brakes more popular at 87-89 percent and power steering at 96-97 percent.

Ford completed the first new production four-passenger Thunderbird on December 20, 1957, and the car made its bow for the public on February 13, 1958—very late for a new

(top) Air conditioning controls for 1958–1960 used a series of pull knobs and levers to open and close valves and doors. Air conditioning was the most expensive option ($465.80) for 1960.

(above) An inboard lens with white center for the back-up light was a $9.50 option in 1960.

(opposite) The 1960 hardtops, such as this Raven Black one, could be ordered with a sliding metal panel sunroof for $212.40.

model introduction. Allowed to see and drive pre-production cars in the late fall of 1957, critics fawned over how different it was from anything else on the road, not only because of its styling but also because of its engineering. *Motor Trend* was so impressed that it gave its third "Car of the Year" award to the four-passenger coupe, but others panned its 3,708-pound bulk and lamented that if only more carburetors or a supercharger could be had, the car would be as fast as it looked. Of course, that's not what McNamara wanted. The design team had planned to use a supercharger with the 352, but that was in May 1957—just as the AMA ban went into effect.

Ford hoped to launch the convertible with the fixed roof car, but bugs in the top system delayed the drop-top's unveiling until June. Planners were anticipating that half of all Thunderbirds would be convertibles. At $3,914 per car, they were overly optimistic: only 2,134 cars were built with the semi-automatic retractable soft top. The assembly nearly filled the 23.2-cubic-foot trunk when lowered, leaving only four cubic feet for luggage. If the purpose of the four-place car was to accommodate families, the complete lack of luggage space with the semi-retractable top rendered that version all but useless for overnight travel.

Ford concluded production on the 1958 T-Bird in September 1958. Novi-Wixom built 37,892 1958 Thunderbirds. Of these, 2,134 were drop-tops—the model buyers had avoided in 1958 has become the most-coveted of the post-classic Thunderbirds. The uptick of nearly 16,000 sales over 1957 proved the Whiz Kid right; people wanted a four-seat Thunderbird. In fact, Thunderbird was a very profitable car for Ford in a year marked with a mild recession. The only other new introduction car that did better was Milt Romney's little Rambler from the conglomerated American Motors Corporation. Once the new parts could be placed on the storage racks and tooling readied for new rear suspensions, the 1959 models could begin to pick up where the 1958 had left off.

The second iteration of the squared-off Thunderbird incorporated several significant additions. The primary one was what the critics had wanted: a larger engine. The monster MEL-series 430-ci engine, initially set aside for Mercury, Lincoln, and the upper-line Edsel, was a 350-horsepower behemoth with a larger Cruise-O-Matic that could take the staggering 490 foot-pounds of torque the engine delivered at 2,800 rpm. It was the largest-displacement engine Ford built for a passenger car until the late 1960s. Officially available only with the cast-iron automatic, a 2.91:1 rear axle for less-than-neck-snapping acceleration, and larger 8.50x14 tires, the 430 was virtually custom-adapted and shoehorned into the T-Bird's engine cavity. Prototypes and one-offs have been documented, but with a manual transmission.

Aside from the suspension change back to rear elliptical leaf springs and some brake line rerouting, Ford didn't change much mechanically. Trim would be the focus of most peoples' attention, starting with the clean look of the horizontal bars in the grille and taillight panels and spear tip on the door windsplit. The fender ornaments had a T-Bird emblem in the center over a black background, and a smaller cast-metal T-Bird emblem

While only one of the original eight Holman-Moody-built Grand National cars survives, the #73 car originally campaigned by the Burdick family of Omaha, Nebraska, was cloned in street-legal form. Original race-prepared cars had no finished interiors, headlights, or other road-worthy items.
Courtesy Wally Warpeha

appeared on hardtop roofs. Exterior colors were expanded with 19 solid colors and 41 two-tones for hardtops. Convertibles could be had with a choice of seven combinations of four exterior colors and four cloth liners. Seating choices included four cloth/vinyl, six two-tone vinyl, and four leather colors with matching-color door and trim panels. The 1959 was a very striking restyle.

As the model year progressed, Ford made updates and modifications in response to service department feedback. Changes including moving the horn from the front wheelwells, where it was exposed to water and road debris. An improved, firewall-mounted brake booster replaced the underdash version unless the 430 or air conditioning was installed. To resolve complaints about having to stand by the trunk to work the convertible top, engineers developed a fully automatic system using relays and a dash-mounted switch. The automatic top advertised in mid-year brochures didn't appear until the 1960 models were released.

Brought out four days before Halloween 1958, the Thunderbird was obscured by the shadows of Sputnik 1 orbiting the earth and the Edsel taking to the streets. What the T-Bird lacked in publicity, it made up for in sales. By the end of September 1959, 67,456 Thunderbirds had satisfied owners, while the Edsels were wanting for buyers. Of the 57,195 hardtop and 10,261 convertible Thunderbirds assembled, 3,154 closed and 1,168 open cars had the large 430.

The 430-engined Thunderbird's sales were most likely helped along because of exposure in a venue that Ford officially had bowed out of—stock car racing. Unknown to McNamara and other powers in the company, a pair of good ol' boys from North Carolina had approached contacts at Wixom in the fall of 1958 and arranged to take a collection of "scrap" parts off their hands. These parts included engines and suspension components from Lincolns, Mercury heavy-duty manual transmissions, and eight damaged, unassigned Thunderbird bodies. Trucked to race car builder Holman-Moody, the shells were worked over to accept the hodge-podge of parts and sold to aspiring speedway race teams. Built without interiors or other niceties, some cars were also set up with bolt-on roofs so they could run in both convertible and closed car classes.

In an arrangement between Holman-Moody, which had bought out Ford's factory racing parts inventory in the summer of 1957, and NASCAR magnate Bill France, the 430-equipped Birds were given special dispensation to run for the 1959 season. Turned loose at the inaugural Daytona 500 race on February 22, 1959, the #73 car owned by the Burdick family of Omaha, Nebraska, and driven by Iowa native Johnny Beauchamp appeared to take the checkered flag ahead of veteran driver and favorite Lee Petty in the #42 Oldsmobile from North Carolina. Three days after a photo finish, the cup was given to Petty and for the next two years, Thunderbirds fought to win. The Birds were most successful in a half-dozen closed and another five convertible races for the 1959 season.

Larger-than-anticipated expenditures to develop the four-place T-Bird ate up the budget for restyling, in part due to work on a gas turbine-powered derivative Ford had been experimenting with beginning in 1955. Trim work was about all that could be done for 1960. Exterior ornamentation became busier. Paired in three groups of three, nine vertical bars adorned the rear quarters. On the door, large, cursive script replaced the more-angular lettering that had been used since 1957. On the other hand, the bird ornaments were simplified with narrow wings and a wider span. Grille and taillight panel treatment incorporated large vertical teeth and a matching horizontal bar over square mesh. Oval gunsights dressed up the front fender tops. Providing background for all the new trim were 19 choices of enamel and 41 possible two-tones for closed cars. For the inside, seat inset patterns changed from pleats to large squares for vinyl and cloth fabrics, while vertical pleats advertised the use of leather. Five cloth/vinyl, six two-tone vinyl, four leather trims, and three convertible tops were available. A polarized glass day-night mirror was now standard equipment. One improvement that didn't receive much attention was the increase of the brake lining area; it was increased to 208 square inches by widening the 11-inch diameter

brake drums and shoes to 2 1/2 inches. The new sticker price was $3,755 for a stripped-down hardtop and $4,222 for a similarly equipped ragtop.

Ford added a third roof option—a sliding metal panel sunroof. The sunroofs were installed offsite under contract with the American Specialty Company (later known as American Sunroof Company or ASC), owned by Heinz Prechter. Designated bodies on their journey from Budd's assembly plant to Wixom were diverted to Prechter's facility and fitted with the sliding roof panel. From there, the bodies continued to Ford's assembly plant for painting and decking. Not given a separate model number, the sunroof Thunderbirds were treated as hardtops except that workers added a separate windbar and stanchions to reduce highway wind noise. The buyer's retail cost for the sunroof was $242.

Those who favored the convertible appreciated its automatic action. The operator loosened the front bow clamps and pulled a handle. The rear deck hinged open from the back, the framework collapsed into the trunk, and a filler panel flipped out from under the deck lid to conceal the gap behind the rear seat. Refinements in the system resulted in the original 10 electro-mechanical relay bank's expansion to 12 relays to cure complaints of battery drain.

The 1960 Thunderbird proved to be the most popular yet. Ford built 92,843 examples from September 8, 1959 through September 13, 1960. Convertibles accounted for a record 11,860 units, and 1,245 had the 430-ci engine. There were 2,536 sunroof versions, of which 377 had the Lincoln engine. The remaining 78,447 closed cars included 3,900 equipped with the 430. Automatic transmissions made their way into 98 percent of all Thunderbirds, with three-speed manual and overdrive cars splitting the remainder. Power brakes and power steering were as common as the automatic transmission.

In the summer of 1960, Budd prepared two hardtops with stainless steel bodies for Allegheny-Ludlum Steel Corporation. Ford trimmed the cars in red leather and equipped them with 352-ci engines and Cruise-O-Matic transmissions. Allegheny-Ludlum representatives drove each car over 100,000 miles throughout the United States, Canada, and overseas to extol the advantages of stainless steel. The company retained the cars in its private collection and restored them at least twice for display at museums.

The second-generation Thunderbird, nicknamed "Squarebird" because of its roofline, has earned a place in automotive enthusiasts' hearts for its styling, solid performance, and size—not too big, not too small.

(opposite) Styling changes for 1960 were limited to ornamentation, such as the hash marks and thin-wing 'Bird emblems on this Monte Carlo Red sunroof.

(left) The open sunroof reveals red leather interior ($106.20 option), power windows ($102.10 option), and air conditioning.

CHAPTER THREE

1961–1963
Speeding Bullet

At $4,637, the 1961 convertible continued to utilize a fully concealed convertible top and a smooth rear deck.

(opposite) The tight quarters between the engine and inner fenders was in anticipation of front wheel drive, which was abandoned after the body's engineering had been finalized.

(above) This Aquamarine and Corinthian White 1961 hardtop reveals the heavy emphasis on projectile-like styling.

(right) For 1961–1963, door handles disappeared and became part of the fins, and a separate push button operated the latch.

(far right) Four small spears on the rear quarter identify 1961 models from the other years.

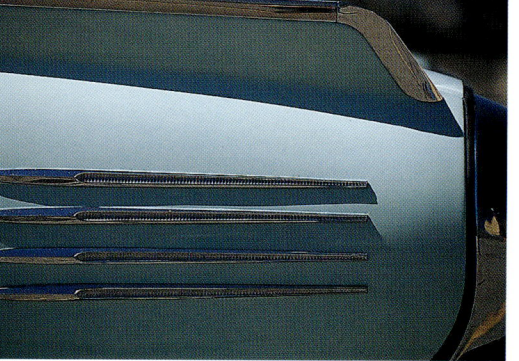

The Thunderbird was an amazing concept for Ford Motor Company. Established as a "loss leader" to draw people into showrooms, it evolved into a successful four-place cruiser. A styling leader, rather than follower, the Thunderbird never wore the big tail fins that sprouted on almost all of its 1950s peers. Merging sports-car image and sedan practicality in a compressed package, it had no equal—a fact duly noted by the competition. Likewise, Ford Division thought the concept warranted expansion.

Ford Division president Robert McNamara had been vindicated in his decision to stretch the original Thunderbird into a four-seater. By 1958, the company was planning the next generation of Fords to usher in the 1960s. The platform nearest to the pragmatic leader's heart, the Falcon, was well along in development. Product planner Tom Case, who had been with the Thunderbird from day one, was now involved with the XK-Bird project, as Falcon was code-named. Donald Peterson, who would become Ford's president in the 1980s, became Thunderbird's new champion to management.

Within Ford Motor Company, the Lincoln-Mercury division coveted the Thunderbird's success. They had had far less luck enticing buyers to the new slant-eyed Lincoln and exorbitantly expensive Mark II. When George Walker, vice president of styling, asked the Thunderbird and Lincoln design teams to compete with one another for the design of the 1961 T-Bird, Lincoln Division gladly accepted the challenge. If their design prevailed, perhaps the 1961 Thunderbird would wear the Lincoln four-pointed star.

Given the generous period of almost four months to explore design concepts and full-size mock-ups, the two groups set off to work. The Ford team, led by Joe Oros, decided to pursue early studies for a projectile-like profile. The Lincoln team, under control of Elwood Engle, went another direction and chose to go formal. By mid-fall 1958, both teams' full-size studies were almost firmed up for final presentation to Henry Ford II, Robert McNamara, and others controlling the decision. The top brass liked both designs—the projectile-like image for the Thunderbird and the slab-sided treatment for the new Lincoln. Lincoln's two-door design was later stretched to accommodate suicide doors.

Lincolns and Thunderbird shared the same cowl and windshield, which helped reduce production costs. They used a similar fender-edge treatment, which employed a pinch-welded lip covered by stainless steel trim. Even the convertible top system would be similar in concept, but utilize different parts. The Thunderbird and Lincoln also reused the same basic engine types used for 1960, except that the Thunderbird did not get the 430; instead, engineers bored and stroked the 352 powerplant to displace 390-ci.

The 390 would become one of Ford's all-time workhorse mills. With a 4.05-inch bore and 3.76-inch stroke, it could make 300 horses at 4,600 rpm and 427 foot-pounds of torque at 4800 revs using hydraulic tappets, a cast-iron intake, and Ford's 4100-series four-barrel carburetion. Teamed with an upgraded Cruise-O-Matic transmission, which allowed starts in first or second gear, the car needed all the torque it could get to spin the 3.10:1 rear axle and propel nearly two tons' worth of metal down the road.

The 1961 Thunderbird used a new front suspension, employing drag struts with a smaller lower control arm. The coil springs mounted on top of the upper control arm and pressed against the upper inner fender instead of residing between the lower arm and spring pocket. The reason for this setup was to create a gap through which half-shafts could be run to the front wheels. The 1961 T-Bird's designers had anticipated a front-wheel drive system becoming available during this generation's production run, but management found anticipated development costs prohibitive. The new suspension, which was already in production, remained. The car's deep-welled inner fender aprons made the cut as well.

Bodies were again unitized, but the front fenders could be unbolted to facilitate repair and replacement, as could the front substructure once some strategic welds were cut. Instead of retaining the integral nose panel and forward-hinged hood that had been used since 1955, designers moved the hinges to the inner fender apron near the cowl, allowing the hood to open from the front for better access to the engine bay. The front bumper formed an anti-climber below the hood edge, framing a cast grille assembly of long, horizontal openings that sloped back and under the nose. With a prow that came to a point, the front end looked like a rocket ship or jet fighter.

The roof retained its characteristic squared-off rear with a slight overhang at the top, and compound-curved glass was used for both front and rear lights. Side glass was also curved to provide more room inside the car. The vent windows had clear plastic deflectors so that they could be opened without the fear of letting too much air or inclement weather inside. The four-foot doors, among the longest in the industry, allowed for easier access to the rear seats. Designers kept the body sides clean by integrating the door handle with the full-length upper body fin. A small push button was nestled into the bodyside curvature to unlatch the door. Ornamentation was limited to the Thunderbird script used for 1957–1959, four small windsplits bolted to the rear quarter, and a new version of the Thunderbird logo on the hood, rear deck lid, and C-pillars. Rear bumpers retained Ford's trademark pair of round lenses, with heavy bumper-stock housings shaped like Qs protecting them from impact. Paint choices expanded to twenty solid colors and over twice the number of two-tones, while convertible tops were again held to three choices.

A tall transmission/driveshaft tunnel again appeared, but the console stopped just behind the bucket seat backs. In back, the rayon loop-pile carpet covered the tunnel. Six color choices with combinations of five cloth/vinyl, six vinyl, and five leather combinations were available. Vinyl-covered panels were molded to go up and over the top of the door structure and to meet the edges of the dash pad, which appeared thinner at the leading edges and more fluid. Again, the radio was located in the center of the pad. The rounded trapezoid placed below the pad and above the heater controls provided an outlet for the integral air conditioner for the 23,815 cars equipped with it. Instruments were placed inside the driver's side in three separate pods: the center pod contained the speedometer; temperature/gas gauges and idiot lights were in the outboard pod; and a clock was in the

(above) Interiors for 1961–1963 reflected a space-age influence with individual pods and ribbed aluminum trim panels.

(left) Little changed on the exterior for 1962, which can be distinguished by the three sets of chrome ornaments on the rear quarter. Single round taillights became larger and had stamped aluminum trim.

(below) The nameplate used on 1957–1959s was used for 1961 and 1962.

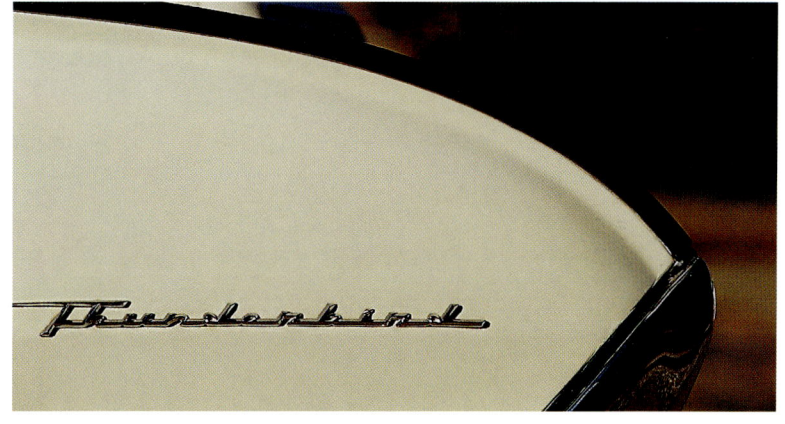

1961-1963

(above) To celebrate the Golden Anniversary of the Indianapolis Motor Speedway, the 1961 T-Bird was selected to be the Pace Car for the Indianapolis 500. One of the original cars was restored to the resemble the number two backup car's configuration. Courtesy Mike Sercer

(right) When production fell behind during and in the aftermath of a month-long work delay, people waiting for their new Thunderbird received this scroll thanking them for their patience while their car was waiting to be assembled. Courtesy Tim Pundt

inboard pod. Separate controls for the cowl vents allowed the driver and passenger to regulate fresh air intake individually.

The Swing-Away steering wheel/column made its debut for 1961. Lifting the shift lever past Park disengaged a latch on the column, allowing it to swing toward the center of the car about 10 inches. At least 77 percent of all Thunderbird buyers for 1961 felt easier ingress and egress was worth the cost of the option. To improve rearward visibility, the interior rear view mirror was mounted on a bracket glued to the windshield—a trick that would become commonplace across manufacturers by the mid-late 1960s. Power windows were installed in over three-quarters of the cars built for the year.

The 1961 Thunderbird debuted the day after Veterans Day, on November 12, 1960—just a week after the presidential election changed Ford's leadership. Robert McNamara had become president of Ford Motor Company in summer 1960, but President-elect John F. Kennedy wanted McNamara for his Cabinet. McNamara denied Secretary of the Treasury, but accepted appointment as Secretary of Defense. To honor Kennedy's inauguration in January 1961, Ford ordered at least 25 Thunderbird convertibles and shipped them to Washington for dignitaries to use at the celebration.

Journalists were in love with the new car. It was fresh, had plenty of power, and turned as many heads as any of the previous models. But there was still a lack of trunk space when the convertible top went down. Steering and handling improved with a new, integral power steering gear using a quicker 20.37-to-1 ratio that did away with the ram cylinder hung off the linkage and frame rails, but was also a source of problems if not assembled properly. The 3,958 pounds of hardtop or 4,130 pounds of convertible were also quite a bit to stop on 11-inch drum brakes that were again increased in area but provided with self-adjusters for the first time. A weak transmission case also played havoc with owners once they'd added some miles, sending many 1961s to an early demise.

In the spring of 1961, Thunderbird was named pace car for the 50th Indianapolis 500

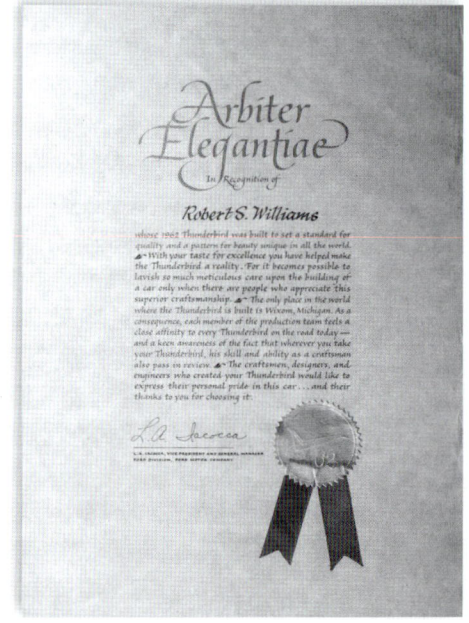

(top) The tonneau cover over the rear seats of this Corinthian White 1963 Sports Roadster created a two-seater look. Wire wheels provided additional flash.

(above left) The rear deck lid ornament for 1961–1963 hid the lock cylinder on closed cars under the 'Bird's head, but it was stationary on convertibles.

(above right) Thunderbird engines with the four-barrel 390 for 1963 had a Castillian Gold-painted air cleaner and valve covers.

and the speedway's 50th anniversary. Ford prepared two cars for primary and backup duties, along with a third as a camera car. Local Ford dealers provided another 33 Birds for parade duty during the Indianapolis 500 Festival preceding the May 30 race. A. J. Foyt took the checkered flag—along with the keys to the primary pace car.

Ford ceased first-year production of the pointy-nosed Thunderbird on August 10, 1961, after building 73,051 cars, including 10,516 convertibles. The T-Bird count was down 19,792 units—a 21-plus percent drop—from 1960. Some attribute the downturn to styling too advanced for the public to accept. Others point to an overall decline in car sales, and the appearance of competing cars for 1961 and 1962 using the bucket seat/personal luxury formula, including the Impala SS, Oldsmobile Starfire, Studebaker Gran Turismo Hawk, and Pontiac Grand Prix.

Styling changed little for 1962. New trim appeared on the quarters and the grille used a stamped aluminum assembly of squares and bars. Inside, additions and deletions raised color choices to seven, available for all seat cover treatments. Five colors were available for cloth/vinyl combinations, 80/20 rayon/nylon carpet was introduced, and the Swing-Away wheel became standard. Exterior color offerings expanded to 21, with multiple two-tone options for the hardtop. Two new models captured enthusiasts' attention: the Landau and Sports Roadster. The Landau featured a padded long-grain vinyl-covered hardtop that emulated old convertibles with a pair of plated S-bars in lieu of the T-Bird emblems. The option added $77 to the hardtop's $4321 base price. Yet, the Sports

Roadster would really steal the show.

Starting with a typical Thunderbird convertible, Ford stylists took direction from vice president Iacocca to create a throwback to the two-seater. By forming a cover out of fiberglass with padded vinyl headrests, placing it over the rear seats, and wrapping it up and over the front seat backs, they created a natural-looking extension of the rear deck lid that was as elegant as it was simple.

(opposite) This Corinthian White 1963 hardtop with optional $26.60 fender skirts, $42.10 optional white sidewall tires, and deluxe wheel covers with simulated knock-off hubs reflects how most cars were delivered.

(left) The hood scoop was lined up with the intake for the air cleaner and was fully functional.

At the four corners, chrome-plated Kelsey-Hayes 48-spoke wire wheels with Ford-designed tribar spinners set in stainless steel pans replaced the steel 14x5.5-inch wheels. The Sports Roadsters had no rear fender shields because the spinners left inadequate clearance. To further embellish the sports concept, the Roadster included a chrome-plated "sissy" bar with a segmented vinyl pad that bolted to the underside of the passenger dash cove. Ford offered the model in only eight colors. Completed with a pair of special emblems on the front fenders and in the center of the tonneau's center leg, the Roadster proved to be another "halo" car for the Thunderbird line. Buyers paid $5,439 for the package, compared to $4,788 for the basic convertible.

Originally handled as special packages on standard models, the Landau and Sports Roadster received separate identification codes by the end of November 1961.

To match the flash of the Sports Roadster, Ford needed more power from the 390-ci engine. Engineers swapped the cylinder heads for those from the 406 engine, installed a camshaft with higher lift and duration, and upped the exhaust system tubes from 1-3/4 to 2 inches in diameter. For added flash, engineering created a new manifold to accept the full-size cars' triple two-barrel carburetion. This new M-series engine cranked out 340 ponies at 5,000 rpm and generated 430 foot-pounds of torque at 3,200 revs.

The Thunderbird Sports V-8, as the M-series was called, used a modified, aluminum oval open-element air cleaner with a small version of the series bird on top, and some chrome dress-up goodies to further distinguish it. To handle the engine's extra power, Ford beefed-up the Cruise-O-Matic transmission.

Less than 10 percent of the Roadsters were optioned with tri-power, and a lesser number of the others were as well. Yet problems with the design caused many owners to remove the triple carbs because they were difficult to keep in tune and could catch fire if left to run rough. Ford did not keep records on how many Thunderbirds were optioned with tri-power. The majority went to buyers in four-barrel guise. Problems in development delayed the Sports V-8 until the end of December 1961. The package received some minor refinements in 1963, primarily the camshaft, and was dropped after the beginning of January 1963.

(above) The 1963 1/2 Limited Edition Monaco Landau had a unique Rose Beige vinyl roof. It was a reddish-brown color that faded terribly in the sun.

(right) Limited Edition Landaus all had special Rosewood dash trim and a numbered plate under the heater controls with the crest of the Principality of Monaco.

60   ***Chapter Three***

The Italien was a concept car built for 1963's auto show circuit, with a fiberglass fastback roof and custom interior. The car was sold to actor Dale Robertson, given to his gardener, and eventually fell into disrepair. Ford Motor Company, Alan H. Tast collection

The Italien featured an oxblood red leather interior and unique interior trim. Ford Motor Company, Alan H. Tast collection

(right) This 1963 hardtop's exterior color is Silver Mink.

(opposite) This detail of the 1962–1963 M-series engine shows the large, oval aluminum open element air cleaner and chrome-plated valve covers.

62　**Chapter Three**

Mid-year changes were plenty for the line. Mid-April brought a major interior revision that smoothed out the upper door panel's contours and widened the dash pad to close the gap between the door panel and the ends of the dash. Manufacturing and finishing changes resulted in firewalls being blacked out instead of painted the body color. Other minor refinements crept in throughout the year.

A company-wide strike during September and October 1961 delayed delivery of all Ford products, including Thunderbirds. Buyers awaiting delivery were provided with parchment certificates in mailing tubes promoting the notion that the Thunderbird was worth the wait, built by fine craftsmen to a higher level of quality. Once the strike was settled, new Roadsters and other models began to flow into dealer lots. Wixom stopped its conveyor belts for 1963 retooling on August 6, 1962, after producing 78,011 examples of the 1962 T-Bird. There had been 68,122 hardtops and Landaus (Ford didn't break out the two models even though they were coded separately), 8,457 convertibles, and 1,427 Sports Roadsters. The early Fords were without separate model designations, and those built in late November 1961 and beyond had the designations of "76B" on the data plate and "89" in the serial number. Ford didn't track total M-series production, but evidence suggests that 120 Roadsters had the special engine. In addition, enthusiasts have documented at least 17 convertibles, 34 hardtops, and 12 Landaus with the M-code option. Buyers proved to be more interested in power windows (75.6 percent of 1962s) and air conditioning (32.6 percent).

Deemed "Unique in all the World," the 1963s brought out for general inspection on September 28, 1962, had a host of mechanical and styling changes. The 1963 was given a facelift with a new saw-toothed grille, hash marks on the doors, and a feature line running from the tip of the front fender to behind the door emblems. The nameplate moved to the rear quarter, just forward of the bumper ends, and a turbine motif was used for the taillight bezels to play off of Ford's ongoing development work with turbine engines. An optional wheel cover for all cars except Sports Roadsters used the wire wheel's center spinner and a black plastic medallion. Color choices were reduced to 20, while interior color selections rose to nine using four cloth/vinyl, nine vinyl, and six leather trims. Vinyl tops were available in dark blue or dark brown, in addition to the prior year's black or white, while convertible top colors remained black, white, or blue.

Engineers made a number of mechanical improvements for 1963. These included replacing the direct-current generator with a more reliable alternator, strengthening the upper front suspension arms and shock absorbers to counter problems with cracking A-frames, and increasing brake surface area and cooling. The integral power steering gear was also redesigned to resolve persistent recall issues during the past year, and a set of rubber-bushed isolators helped to keep road vibration from traveling up to the steering wheel.

Inside, an AM/FM radio and rear seat speaker joined the options list. To make hearing it easier, designers added more padding and sound deadener to the floor pans, trunk, and quarter panel cavities. Seat covers got an all-new pattern that draped over the top of the seatbacks, and door panels now had courtesy/warning lights in the bottom. Landaus got walnut-grained interior trim panels instead of the ribbed aluminum ones used for the past two years. Air conditioning was installed in 43.5 percent of all 1963s, and 70.9 percent got power windows.

To test the waters of future Thunderbird styling, the Design Center developed a fastback version of the third generation for display at auto shows. Called the "Italien," the show car was a 1962 convertible, gutted and given a new fiberglass roof with slanted backlight, oxblood red leather seat covers, and other novel accents inside a maroon-colored shell. The car dazzled crowds but Ford chose not to put it into production. The car survived and today awaits restoration.

The crowning achievement for the model was the Limited Edition "Princess Grace" or "Monaco" Landau, for which actress-turned-monarch Grace Kelly provided styling input. Ford's marketing people got the idea for the special car as a tie-in for the T-Bird promoting the Ford Falcon Rally team's effort in the Monte Carlo Rally held in early 1963. Princess Grace agreed to participate, and she and her staff helped determine color choices and other touches. The special Landaus were finished in Corinthian White with a burgundy-colored vinyl roof, unique white appointments, including steering wheel, leather seats, and door panels, with mouton-colored carpeting and rose-beige dash trim.

The cars were identified with a serial-numbered plate on the dash from one to 2000 over simulated rosewood panels.

Close of production on July 17, 1963, marked the end of an era for the Thunderbird. Ford built 63,313 of the 1963 model—42,806 hardtops, 12,139 regular Landaus, 5,913 convertibles, and 455 Sports Roadsters. Only 37 Sports Roadsters were documented with the M-code option, which was dropped mid-run. Though Ford did not retain records on the other examples, collectors and enthusiasts have identified at least 28 convertibles, 27 hardtops, and 22 Landaus with the M-code engine (it was not available on the Monaco). Most likely, there were more and some no doubt await discovery in salvage yards, garages, and wooded lots.

The Riviera was GM's first true direct competition for the Thunderbird, and its initial showing of 40,000 sales cut into the Thunderbird's formerly exclusive domain. The Pontiac Grand Prix and Oldsmobile Starfire also hurt Thunderbird, but Ford's own Galaxie 500/XL and Mercury Monterey S-55-series cars probably stole some of the thunder as well. Other challengers would soon appear, including a little pony.

The 1963-1965 Buick Riviera (1965 shown) was purpose-built to compete head-to-head with the Thunderbird. The Riviera had bucket seats, a full-length console, and a large engine.
John Lee

CHAPTER FOUR

1964–1966
Rolling Sculpture

The projectile look was still popular at the time this Samoan Coral 1964 hardtop was built, but door handles reverted to being separate castings.

(opposite) The hardtop received a new version of the Thunderbird emblem. Landaus used an S-bar and an oval center.

(right) The 1964 squared-off rear pontoons were a very handsome design.

For an additional $103, a person could step up from the base hardtop to a vinyl-roofed Landau, such as this Florentine Green and White version with optional deluxe spinner wheel covers.

Chapter Four

From the beginning, Thunderbird styling had been influenced by jet planes and rockets, with pointed noses that suggested missile nose cones; hood scoops that mimicked jet engine air intakes; taillights that resembled jet exhaust nozzles; and fins that overtly reflected wings, rudders, and wind strakes. Some of the cues had been subtle, others very obvious. The imagery was fun to play with, almost gimmicky. The question for the design team was how far down the aeronautical pathway buyers would be willing to go.

Thunderbird's designers began planning the fourth generation during the late months of 1960. They already had the third generation set in steel, with advanced production of 1962 parts underway, and the 1963's facelift on their desks. To produce a new model for fall 1963 introduction, the departments involved needed two full years to generate a concept, coordinate engineering and design efforts, develop prototypes, and set up tooling for production components. To ensure adequate testing, they would need prototypes by late 1962 and early 1963.

The company explored four directions for the car. One employed front-wheel drive—then in working prototype form for possible use in the 1963 Thunderbird. Two similar ideas involved an all-new body on a stretched wheelbase to permit sharing parts with the Lincoln Continental. The fourth avenue was to re-skin the 1961-series and retain its substructure. With Robert McNamara still on board at Ford, the nod went to the facelift. It would be quicker to build and evaluate, as well as less expensive to bring to market. Therefore, it would generate a higher profit margin.

Styling work on the car began in the winter of 1961 and carried through the next 18 months. Package dimensions were to be virtually the same as the 1961–1963 models, with an overall length of 205.4 inches; the width gained almost five-eighths of an inch to reach 77.1 inches. Initial studies played with retaining the 1963's rounded quarters and tail with a variety of different front clips, but none of the stylings looked attractive. Another looked at melding the rear of the Lincoln with a revised 1963 front end, but they didn't look good together. By the summer of 1961, the look was finally taking shape to a point where interior work could begin.

The designers retained and updated the Thunderbird themes of dual-pontoon rears and pointed front ends. The bumper retained its anti-climber bar at the top, while a separate chrome-plated bottom chin was used, with two individual bumper guards protecting the grille. Turn signals were set into the bottom of the assembly rather than recessed into the grille. Flattening the rear, depressing the center section similar to the Squarebirds, and installing rectangular taillights with a pinched center for a plastic emblem spelling out the car's name, produced a wider, more contemporary look. The wide taillights also provided an opportunity to try out a concept car idea for signals that flashed in sequence in the direction the driver intended to turn. To handle the added electrical draw from six taillights, and stop the brake lights from overloading and failing, engineers added a relay to regulate the current fed to the tail. The final touch was to put the turn indicators in small chrome housings on the front fenders, rather than on the dash. Despite the system's elegance, traffic safety authorities had some reservations on the new lights, so Ford put them on hold until the next model year.

(below) Samoan Coral, also known as Bittersweet, was only offered on the T-Bird and was one of six colors originally available with the Sports Tonneau Cover option.

The body sides and roof for hardtops and Landaus became straighter, with highlights splayed out forward of the rear door jamb. Hash marks were dropped, while the 1963 script was reused and moved to the front fender. Thunderbird logos on the roof sides of hardtops introduced a new design without plastic inserts. The flattened rear deck lid had a pentagon-shaped cover with a body-painted insert to protect the

(above) For 1965, little was changed on the outside from the previous year.

(right) Major distinguishing features for 1965 include a modified roof emblem with a framed body, faux front fender air extractor, and script emblem on rear quarter. The stainless-steel body side molding was a $17.15 option, and fender skirts added $32.70.

(above) The first year for sequential taillights was 1965—ten years after the Thunderbird's introduction—and it carried the T-Bird's spirit of innovation forward.

(left) Brittany Blue was carried over for 1965 as one of 22 colors offered that year.

(below) Instead of being in the dash, the turn signal indicators were moved to the front fenders in bullet-shaped pods.

trunk lock cylinder. For the first time, a series of block letters spelled out the car's name on the hood, with the trademark scoop retained but non-functional. Color choices grew to 23. Ford also added two new colors in mid-year, while deleting two others. Hardtop buyers could choose from at least 19 two-tone schemes.

Thunderbird interiors had become an integral part of the cars' innovative styling. For the fourth generation, Interior Design Studio head, Art Querfeld, decided to break away from the twin-pod motif used so successfully for the past two generations and tie together the two halves of the car. While still working with a high transmission tunnel, Querfeld's team took the dash pad across the width of the cowl and gave it a deep, hooded effect. Taking inspiration from aircraft cockpits, with wall-to-wall instruments and levers, they placed oil pressure, coolant temperature, fuel level, and ammeter in separate pods. Operating controls for wipers, vents, and map lights went into a pod suspended from the underside of the dash pad, and the clock was housed in its face. Below the pod, an optional set of toggle switches activated vacuum door locks. A new safety feature allowed parking lights to flash in unison in an emergency, along with its interior indicator light. Another small light illuminated if fuel levels dropped below an eighth of a tank. The novel speedometer arrangement played on linear themes by providing a narrow view slot, behind which a rotating drum created an illusion of a red-orange line that got longer as the car went faster.

The Mustang provided many of the Thunderbird's attributes in a smaller package, and as a result, ate into T-bird sales. Alan H. Tast

The top of the console was trimmed with a brushed aluminum appliqué on hardtops and convertibles, or a faux walnut finish in Landaus. It wrapped up and across the front of the driver to contain the radio, heater control head, light and ignition switches, and the swing-away column opening. Half of the cars had an additional cutout for the air-conditioner outlets. Again, three quarters of T-Birds had power window switches in the console top. If the car was a convertible, the top switch was located below the heater controls in place of the Silent-Flo ventilation switch.

Ford made several seat changes, including a new, reclining passenger seat with adjustable headrest. Buyers had a new high of ten color choices for vinyl seats, but only four in cloth/vinyl and five in leather. The Department of Transportation now mandated front seatbelts, an option since 1955. A reminder light in the console reminded people to "buckle up." Occupants had to push on the skinny red lens to turn the light off.

(above) An original Rangoon Red 1964 hardtop illustrates the balance of proportions between the grille, body, and roof.

(left) The 1964-1965s grille treatment with a deep overhang and high upper bar became a target for federal regulators when maximum height standards were implemented by 1966.

(right) The Palomino show car from 1965 was used to gauge public reaction to future Thunderbird styling, including the Town-style roof. Ford Motor Company

(below) This is an advertisement for the 1965 Special Landau. Alan H. Tast collection

Across the expanse between the seats and rear deck, the panel dropped down in the center for an optional rear seat speaker, and sloped up to provide for another Thunderbird innovation for closed cars—flow-through ventilation. The system allowed air from the interior to be drawn out through an open grille casting at the base of the rear window. After a few years, however, the plenum collected debris, and the drain tubes would clog as well as develop leaks. Wet trunks were a problem with these cars, and rust in the lower trunk area is not uncommon. Convertibles didn't have this, but water seeping into the compartment was still an issue. The other convertible issue was a lack of trunk space; the spare tire was moved into the deep floor well just for this model, meaning that the 11.5-cubic-foot. volume was quickly eaten up when the top went down.

The Sports Roadster was still very much alive in 1963 when Querfeld and John Najjar developed a new version of the tonneau for 1964. This design featured padded headrests and extended the vinyl cover back over the top of the fairings, trimmed with stainless steel edging. When sales were below 500 units for the 1963 version, Ford decided not to market a separate model for 1964 and made the tonneau a factory- or dealer-installed option in limited color choices. The 14-inch Kelsey-Hayes chrome-plated wire wheels and 8.00x14 whitewall tires became an option for all models. Special emblems and a grab bar made it into the shop manual, but not into production. While hundreds of buyers chose the tonneau or the wire wheels, only 45 documented cars left Ford for dealerships with both features installed.

Suspension and running gear was pretty much carried over from the 1963 version, as well as cross-ribbed drum brakes on all four corners. Critics found the brakes weak for a car

weighing 4,195 pounds for a hardtop and 4,586 for a Landau, but overall the car was a big success. Ford produced 92,465 examples—9,198 convertibles (including the Sports Roadsters), 22,715 Landaus, and 60,5252 hardtops. It proved a sales record Thunderbird would not surpass for 13 years.

Front discs for 1965 resolved complaints about the prior year's braking. The hefty units employed four separate pistons to press friction pads against a cross-ventilated cast iron rotor. The design decreased stopping distance and virtually eliminated repetitive-use brake fade. The sequential turn signals originally intended for the previous year were now legal in all 50 states and ready for production. Another novel idea that would become a Ford trademark was the double-sided key. Color selections remained at 23 for the exterior with at least 24 two-tones. Interior colors exploded with the combination of white seats and trim panels coordinated with all the nine other color choices for a total of 65 choices.

To distinguish a 1965 from a 1964, stylists added a set of false air extractors to the front fenders and moved the new rendition of the nameplate to the rear quarter panel. The winged bird emblem returned to the hood, while a surround for the body was added to the roof ornaments on the hardtop, while the S-bar was redone to incorporate the same texture as the long-grained vinyl roof cover. Taillights lost their Thunderbird emblems and now wore a chrome grille. The taillights were so well done that two years later, Ford stylists in conjunction with Shelby American would adapt them for use on the GT350 and GT500s, as well as on such Mustang classics as the California and High Country Specials for 1968. The trademark emblem would move into the bumper center's plastic insert.

(above left) The 1965 Special Landau was introduced mid-year for T-Bird's 10th anniversary and featured either an Emberglo or Wimbledon White body, Parchment vinyl roof and interior, and several other additions for an extra $49.60 over the typical Landau.

(above) The 1965 Special Landau came with deluxe wheel covers that had Emberglo-colored vanes.

Chapter Four

Inside, trim insert panels were changed for the hardtop to a camera-case finish on the console and across the lower dash panel. Other changes provided for optional power antenna, a dome light on the rear bow of the convertible top, and motorized vent windows. Most cars had power windows and a little over half had air conditioning. A vacuum-operated trunk release was available for closed cars. Interior color combinations were multiplied by the addition of white vinyl or leather seat covers in conjunction with the other colors used in the cockpit. Wire wheels were not carried over, as the wires could not be adapted to fit over the disc brake calipers. The tonneau cover, though not available from the factory or promoted in dealer sales literature, could still be ordered at the dealer's parts counter.

Since 1965 would be the tenth anniversary for the Thunderbird line, planners and designers worked to create another limited edition model as a spring sales-inducer. The Special Landau featured a unique reddish-copper Emberglo or Wimbledon White body with Emberglo exterior and interior accents, and a Parchment-colored vinyl roof, seat, and interior trim. Burled walnut appliqués were used on the door panels and console/dash trim, and "Special Landau" emblems were installed. Buyers even got a personalized dash plaque with the car's serialized number from 1-4500.

By the mid-1960s, horsepower was growing, along with other sources of competition. The revamped Riviera in Gran Sport trim offered buyers a dual-quad engine with 360 horses, while the new Mustang was dominating headlines and showrooms. Sales of the 1965 were down 19,493 units from the year before, for a total of 74,493 Thunderbirds. The hardtop was by far the most popular model with 42,652 examples, while the Landau

(opposite) For 1966, the front end received considerable attention. This Silver Rose Metallic convertible is an example of how the bumper and lower front valance changed. Tonneau covers were popular on 1965 and 1966 models, but weren't a factory option.

(below opposite) The last year for a convertible Thunderbird was 1966.

(below) Ford painted all engines Corporate Blue beginning in 1966. The radiator cap is an aftermarket replacement.

accounted for 20,974 (not including the Special Landau's 4500). Convertibles continued their downhill slide, with 6,846 produced.

In 1966, the market fragmented further as more players emerged on the personal luxury scene. Oldsmobile took advantage of Ford's abandoned front wheel drive program in the early 1960s; the company secured the rights to use patents developed in Dearborn for a fraction of their development cost. Ford Motor Company also agreed not to pursue FWD design for a full decade. The new car, named Toronado, was a landmark engineering achievement for Oldsmobile, and it snagged *Motor Trend*'s Car of the Year honors. At the same time, Buick's Riviera underwent its first major restyle and came out with a narrow grille housing, retractable headlights, tilt steering, and a choice of bench or bucket seats. Toronado's 40,963 sales, along with 45,348 for the Riviera, signaled a growing challenge to the Thunderbird's dominance among personal luxury cruisers.

In response to the challengers, in 1964 product planners asked designers to come up with a more formal-looking body to distinguish the 'Bird from the new Riviera and other contenders. Unveiled for the 1965 car show season, the Palomino concept car included rocker panel moldings, segregated taillights, a painted lower front valance, and a blind-quarter roof side that eliminated the B-pillar glass. Public response was overwhelmingly favorable, so management gave the new car—designated the Town series—the green light for tooling.

A lower-priced Town Hardtop model without a vinyl roof at $4,451, and a higher-trimmed Town Landau with a levant-grain vinyl roof and S-bars at $4,552, offered things that the standard five-window hardtop didn't. One big difference was the overhead roof console, which contained elements of the Safety Convenience Control Panel otherwise mounted below the clock pod. The headliner was a molded set of panels composed of vinyl fused to a foam and hardboard backing instead of sewn-together material hung off of steel bows. Side windows were curved to provide a smooth transition and angled back to give passengers head clearance when entering the back seat. As the new kids on the block, Town models drew more attention than the other models, and scored a one-two punch for the year's sales. Town Landaus proved to be the most popular Thunderbird for the year, accounting for half of all models sold at 35,105 examples, and the Town Hardtop drew 15,633 takers. Now the lowest-priced Thunderbird at $4,395, the standard hardtop saw a major decline in popularity with only 13,389 spoken for.

The Town Landau/Town Hardtop weren't the only changes that got people excited about the new Thunderbird. To meet new bumper height requirements, designers took some cues from Mustang in restyling the front end. The lower chrome-plated bumper chin, a holdover from Ford's philosophy from the 1940s and 1950s of not using sheet metal at the lower extremities, was finally abandoned. In its place, designers fitted a sheet metal valance with integrated turn signals. A diecast grille with a pronounced overhang and a very detailed Thunderbird emblem with turquoise plastic inserts called attention to the new face, as did the hood with its de-emphasized power dome and faux intake casting. Fender tops had the

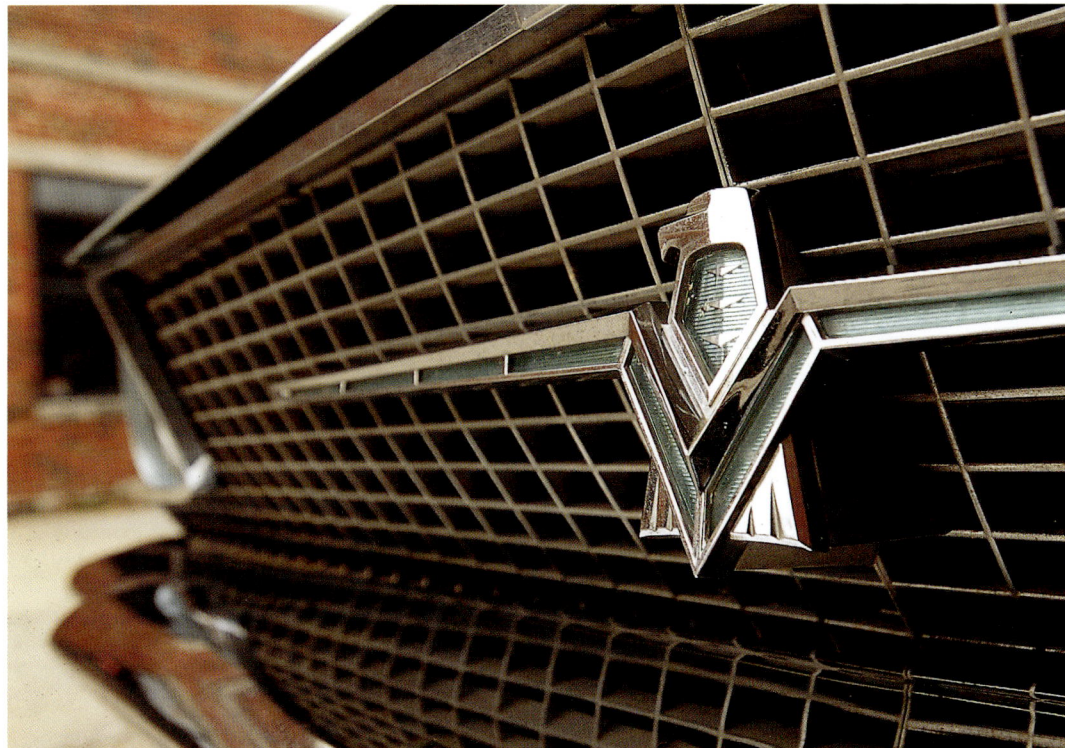

(above) The Town Landau, like this Silver Mink and Black example, was introduced in 1966 as the high-end closed T-Bird.

(left) The thin-blade bumper for 1966 provided an opportunity to revamp the grille and show off a very detailed ornament.

Oldsmobile's Toronado brought front-wheel-drive (FWD) back to American highways. Its drive system owed its beginnings to Ford's aborted development of FWD for Thunderbird in the early 1960s. Courtesy Oldsmobile Historical Archives

windsplits of the past few years shaved off, and windshield wipers received a satin finish to tone down their look. At the rear, wall-to-wall taillights with the backup light now located in the center made an elegant statement. There were now 22 exterior color choices with 34 two-tones for Town hardtops and the five-window versions were available. Addition of Parchment to the two-tone interior selections and reduction of seats available with leather covers provided for 65 interior choices.

Performance enthusiasts finally had reason to celebrate. Ford's engineers took the 390's FE block, bored it out to 4.13 inches, and stroked the crank to 3.98 inches. The resulting 428-ci powerplant used an externally balanced crankshaft and a mild cam with hydraulic lifters to produce 345 horses at 4,600 rpm and 462 foot-pounds of torque at 2,800 rpm. Although Ford didn't keep track of how many 1966 models got the optional engine, best estimates from owner registries and enthusiast databases suggest between 25 and 33 percent.

Behind the upgraded big-blocks, Ford had a new automatic transmission—the cast aluminum C-6, which was both lighter and more robust than its predecessors. All 428s were provided with it, while 390-equipped cars had to wait until November 1965, when production caught up to demand. The C-6 retained Ford's "Green Dot" Cruise-O-Matic shift pattern, which enabled drivers to start out in Low and work up the scale when the selector was placed on a green dot, or start from second and work up to third when put on a white dot.

Even though the convertible body style was an advantage for Thunderbird over its immediate competition, factors inside and outside of Ford's control brought its demise. Ford planners knew as early as 1964, when work on the 1967 Thunderbird began, that the writing was on the wall for the open car. Federal regulators were examining roll-over survival rates, which were low in soft tops without a roll bar. Insurance companies were increasing premiums because of vandalism to convertible tops. Air conditioning was also taking off in popularity, reducing the advantage of an open car in warm weather. Between 1964 and 1966, Thunderbirds produced with air conditioning rose from half to almost 64 percent. Plus, the phenomenally successful Mustang was drawing away open-air drivers who didn't want a huge boat to pilot around town when a more-nimble four-place pony car could do the job. Lack of trunk space with the top down was just another nail in the coffin. When production ceased on June 10, 1966, Ford phased out the fascinating convertible whose mechanism had roots in the 1957 Skyliner. Sales numbers reinforced the decision: Ford built only 5,049 convertibles, less than ten percent of the 69,176 total Thunderbirds.

Thunderbird had come a long way in a dozen years. It was firmly entrenched as an icon in American motoring culture, and regarded as a milestone car with its melding of performance, luxury, and compact size. However, its body was tired, outdated, and expensive to produce. Continuing to stretch more life out of it would have been a sure bet for diminishing returns on investment, especially with all the new cars coming up against it.

CHAPTER FIVE

1967–1969
Mature for Its Age

Chapter Five

A four-door Landau, such as this Pewter Mist Metallic specimen with a black Levant grain roof, was introduced for 1967.

(opposite) The four-door took advantage of rear-hinged back doors as a novel styling cue, which it shared with full-size Lincolns.

Ford's three-year styling cycle called for a new Thunderbird to be in showrooms for 1967. With the necessary lead time for design studies, engineering development, prototype construction, and testing, this meant that work on an all-new design would have to begin literally at the same time that its predecessor generation first hit the streets. At the same time, the Thunderbird was facing an identity crisis. Its formula for success was being knocked off by virtually all the other domestic car companies. And its sibling, the Mustang, had stolen its place as Ford's sporting four-seater. To survive into the 1970s, the T-Bird had to stake out some new ground.

The man to guide its new direction was the same visionary behind the Mustang's tremendous success—Ford's vice president–Car and Truck Group, Lido A. "Lee" Iacocca. The cigar-wielding executive seemed to know what the public craved. With the convertible body style put to rest, Iacocca and others saw a new way to attract more buyers: offer a four-door. The decision solidified the T-Bird's shift from a sporty car to a more subtle, roomier, "image" automobile.

The new Thunderbird was to be made in two versions: a two-door hardtop with a unique, horizontal-sliding B-pillar window, and the four-door hardtop. With the latter, the design team had problems making adequate clearance for the rear doors. The answer was to hinge them on the rear edge. The resulting suicide door gave the four-door T-Bird unique styling among its competitors and allowed it to share rear door parts with the Lincoln.

The new car reverted to separate body and chassis construction to reduce fabrication and assembly costs. Designers reused the four-piston disc brake setup from 1965–1966, but with a dual master cylinder separating front and rear circuits in case of a failure somewhere in the system. The full-size Ford's drag-strut setup supported the front wheels and brakes. Since the fender aprons no longer supported the suspension, the coil spring was sandwiched between a pocket in the frame and lower suspension arm. For the rear axle, a direct-acting three-link coil suspension similar to the 1958 model's helped hold the wheels to the ground and the car off the axles.

The front end of the 1967 series was simplicity itself. Led by veteran Ford designers, L. David Ash and Bill Boyer—both of whom had played great roles in previous Thunderbird incarnations—stylists worked on four different concepts simultaneously and looked to past studies going back as far as the mid-1950s for inspiration. Boyer's Ferrari-inspired recessed grille opening used hidden headlights

(above) The front grille for 1967 featured a large ornament and hidden headlights.

(opposite) Bucket seats and the large padded center hub in the steering wheel (on cars without speed control) were standard for 1967.

The Buick Riviera was restyled in 1966 with few refinements for the 1967 edition shown here. The Riv was neck-and-neck with Thunderbird sales throughout the 1960s. Alan H. Tast collection

and an egg-crate lattice to stretch across virtually the entire width of the front end—similar to the Buick Riviera restyle for 1966, of which the Ford stylists had some knowledge.

To the sides of the cars, the stylists fitted bright aluminum moldings not only along the rocker panels, but to the bottom of front and rear fenders, too. (While distinctive, restorers appreciate this feature less today due to moisture and dirt that collected behind the moldings and created ideal rusting conditions.)

Inside, designers stuck with the previous generation's formula of individual bucket seats, console, and covered rear seats. They created unique door handle latches using a ball-tipped lever in the armrests rather than the typical panel-mounted handle. Four recessed pods held instruments, and a rectangular housing contained slide controls for the vent and wiper controls. A rectangular, brushed-aluminum panel on the passenger side housed air conditioner vents and featured the Thunderbird script. A steering wheel that tilted up and toward the center replaced the previous generation's swing-away column. A padded center hub protruded from the standard steering wheel, while cars with cruise control reused

(above) The Abercrombie & Fitch Apollo began life as a 1967 Thunderbird hardtop and was modified with a powered sunroof, mobile telephone, color TV, reading lamps, and other luxury items. Courtesy Gene Martini/John Ryan

(left) The Apollo hardtops were fitted with a host of luxury items for the day, including a color TV made by Ford's Philco Division. Courtesy Gene Martini/John Ryan

(above) Wall-to-wall taillights were abandoned for 1969, and the back-up lights were hidden in the center panel.

(right) Personal tastes often make their way into older Thunderbirds, such as the 1969 hardtop with wire wheels and custom pinstripes.

(below) Original interiors were monochromatic and somewhat dull. Owner-modified bucket seats and dash were given powder blue accents to brighten up the interior.

the 1966 Highway Pilot single-bar wheel. An overhead console housed indicator lights for the emergency flashers, low-fuel level, and seatbelt reminder. As part of the Convenience Group option, the two-doors got a full-length overhead console similar to the 1966 Town models, but the four-door had a truncated version that also concealed the sun visors. The floor console lacked the previous generation's elevated, padded armrest (this would be corrected for 1968), while the ashtray moved to the flat area between the rear and new forward storage compartment—which was just the right size for 8-track tape storage behind a hinged door with the Thunderbird logo.

The 9 interior color offerings allowed for 25 possible choices between cloth and vinyl, vinyl, or leather seats. The choices included the SL interior, available in either cloth or leather with a quilted rectangular pattern and embroidered accents as an upgrade over the standard vertically pleated vinyl seats. The unique bright-red vinyl was only offered in two-door hardtops. The cloth and leather seats were offered with a reclining passenger seat, while only the black and parchment colors had the reclining passenger seat in vinyl. The leather interior was available only in black. For the car's exterior, buyers could choose any one of 19 colors, including 11 metallic choices. The two- and four-door Landaus offered a Levant-grained vinyl roof in black, white, dark green, or dark brown vinyl.

Options were much the same as before, with a few improvements. One was an AM/FM radio, now stereo, with speakers in the door panels. The reclining passenger seat with adjustable headrest was again offered, as was a vacuum-operated trunk release and cruise control. A shoulder strap for front-seat passengers' seatbelts anticipated their mandatory use the following year. A new vacuum-operated system even locked the doors when the car reached 8 miles per hour, but this was so problem-prone that Ford instructed dealers to deactivate it when cars came in for warranty work; the system was abandoned mid-production. Front and rear seatbelts were now standard, as required by federal law. The rubber-tipped front fender-top ornaments with a raised Vee-bird emblem were very rare. This option appeared only on early cars, but was quickly deleted. Dress-up items included an optional wheel cover with a three-bar spinner, recessed to keep safety-conscious regulators happy, and a simulated five-spoke mag wheel design. Gone for good from the option list were rear fender shields. Wheel arches were open to show off the choice of either narrow whitewall tires or whitewalls with a narrow red accent band.

To their credit, the designers and engineers managed to develop a package that maintained the previous generations' overall proportions and yet also shed a few pounds. The four-door version weighed 38 pounds less than the previous hardtop version, tipping the scales at 4,348 pounds. The two-door version was even lighter, dropping another 92 pounds. Dimensions were fractionally larger, with length increasing from 205.4 inches to 206.9 for both two-and four-door variants, while the car's 77.3-inch width was less than a quarter inch wider. Space between the front and rear wheels revealed the difference between the two models. To improve opening dimensions for the rear door, the frame and driveshaft were lengthened 2.4 inches beyond the two-door's 114.7 inches.

The base model hardtop for 1969 with rocker panel moldings, side marker and cornering lights, and optional multi-bladed wheel covers illustrates the move to restrained use of trim by the end of the 1960s.

The new car's stance was also slightly taller. For 1966, the hardtop stood at 52.5 inches; for 1967, this would increase to 53.8 inches for the four-door and to 54.6 inches for the two-door. The difference between the two models was in part due to the larger 8.45x15-inch tires, which came standard on the four-door, versus 8.15x15-inchers on the two-door if it didn't have air conditioning.

Under the hood, the venerable FE-series duo of the 390- and 428-ci engines returned virtually unchanged. Fuel delivery was revamped with a new four-barrel carburetor, the Autolite 4300-series. Designers also updated the cooling system by returning the filler neck to the radiator, eliminating the expansion tank used since 1958. Thermactor emissions control equipment was carried over from 1966 and mandatory for cars sold in California. The increased air needed to feed the smog-reduction system required a pair of grilles mounted in the lower bumper valance panel. The C-6 slushbox transferred power to the drive wheels. Pulling up the rear was a choice of either a 9- or 9-3/8-inch differential, both with a 3.00:1 drive ratio standard.

Ford formally unveiled the all-new 1967 Thunderbird on September 30, 1966. The automotive pundits weren't overly impressed with the new T-Bird, but potential buyers were satisfied well enough that sales for the 1967 model improved, though not dramatically. A total of 77,976 were built by the end of June 1967, an improvement of 12.7 percent. The four-door accounted for 24,967, falling in the middle of the three model offerings. The two-door hardtop had the fewest takers at 15,567, while the most popular was the vinyl-roofed Landau at 37,422 models.

Even with all the care and attention lavished on development of the car, it had its teething problems like any other first-year offering. Actually, there were quite a few problems—so many that factory orders by April were off by over a third from the 9,182 unit production high of January 1967. So many problems were uncovered that Ford embarked on a special program to resolve owner complaints and rectify them. Ford gave dealers a large three-ring binder full of checklists and procedures for items to correct, including the rolling door locks, and the heating and air conditioning system.

No special edition cars were built for 1967 that could be considered rare or collectible, at least no special editions marketed directly by Ford. There were exceptions, five of them actually, which have become highly desirable. Commissioned by high-end retailer Abercrombie and Fitch in the summer of 1966, five completed two-door Landaus were sent from the Wixom Assembly Plant directly to Ford's custom fabricator of choice, Dearborn Steel Tubing, for some additional modification work. To capitalize on the developing manned space program's effort to reach the Moon, the cars were given the moniker "Apollo."

A host of changes were made on the car to impress the readers of the department store's Christmas season catalog. Starting with a matching dark blue metallic body, vinyl roof, and leather interior, little touches such as gold-plated exterior emblems and chrome-plated door jambs, were accentuated by big items like a powered sunroof, built-in television, mobile telephone with a large V-like antenna on the rear deck lid, and custom rear console with reading lamps on flexible necks. While a base-model Thunderbird hardtop could be had for $4,603, the Apollo Thunderbirds demanded nearly four times that at $15,000. Destined for display prior to their delivery to buyers at the store's five swank locations in New York, Chicago, Miami, Palm Beach, and San Francisco, only four of them made it intact. The San Francisco car was irreparably damaged in transit, and the remaining examples were eventually spoken for. Today at least three of them are still around.

Complaints from owners and warranty recalls probably had a lot to do with changes made for 1968, but most of the cosmetic changes were already set by the beginning of 1967. Many of the changes were government mandated, such as the side marker lights, which were tastefully incorporated into the front fenders along with optional cornering lights and rear quarter panel emblems that had the nameplate reduced to fit in a plastic lens. Shoulder straps on the seatbelts were also required for front seat passengers, but few used them because they were awkward. Another safety innovation required by law was a collapsible steering column.

(opposite) The 1969 Grand Prix was adapted from GM's B-body platform with a stretched wheelbase, which provided a mid-range personal luxury car to compete with the T-Bird. Bunkie Knudsen wanted to shrink the T-Bird's proportions, but it was prevented due to budget constraints. Alan H. Tast collection

Windshield washers, which were a Thunderbird standard issue item since 1964, were now required by law. The windshield wipers were still hydraulically driven, but now they swept across the windscreen in parallel. The driver's side arm incorporated linkage to clean more area by allowing it to pivot as it moved up in the arc. To the back, a blower motor and fan under the package tray blew air against the back light as part of an optional defogger, partially in response to government moves to require them in coming years.

Mechanical refinements were numerous. Disc brakes were simplified to a single-piston, floating caliper design. The cooling fan was now an aluminum flex-fan assembly with blades that flattened out as speed increased. The driveline utilized Cardan-type universal joints, also known as constant-velocity joints, to help reduce issues with noise, vibration, and harshness.

Most noticeable was what was now under the hood. A new engine type, the 385-series, was introduced in the form of the 429-ci Thunderjet V-8. Utilizing the same thin-wall casting technology used in the small-block 289-ci V-8, the new big-block torque-monster produced a rating of 480 foot-pounds at 2,800 rpm on premium gas, 18 more than the 428. Horsepower was rated at 340 at 5,400 rpm, which was lower than the 428's 345 horsepower at 4,600 rpm. Part of the horsepower drop was due to more pollution control equipment, a requirement that took hold at the beginning of the model year. Originally designated as an option over the standard 390-ci engine, it would become the only one offered after the beginning of January.

Outside, the front bumper's lower valance was now painted sheet metal instead of heavy chrome-plated steel to match the bumper bar. The grille was given a more pronounced pattern, and the center-mounted large T-Bird emblem was exchanged for two smaller ones in plastic lenses that were surrounded with a chrome frame. The rear taillights had a similar change, with the two small Birds from 1967 becoming one big, center emblem. For the Landau, vinyl roof material changed from the pebbly Levant grain to Cayman, an alligator-type grain that would be used through the early 1970s.

Interior changes were more pronounced. The instrument control panel now had five round openings instead of four. The added opening was for the wiper and vent controls, doing away with the lever actuators from 1967. Calling attention to the trademark sequential turn signals, indicator lights directly above the steering column and a T-Bird-shaped high-beam indicator light came on in 1-2-3 fashion, just like the lights in the back panel, but just for this year. The passenger side of the dash no longer featured the rectangular opening; a round ventilation outlet that had a small T-Bird fob in the center replaced it. Door handles were moved to the sides of the armrest bases and now used a paddle-like pull. Power window switches were moved to the driver's door armrest, since the console was no longer offered to mount them in standard trim.

The same line-up of radios was offered again, with control knobs both offset to one side. Ford played this up as a safety feature, but it proved a nuisance for owners who wanted to upgrade the sound system. Cut-pile carpeting replaced the looped construction used in previous years. And, most importantly, the trademark bucket seats and console became options instead of standard features. Almost 45 percent—29,199 of all T-Birds sold for 1968—came with the bucket seats. Now the base choice for front seating was a bench with a fold-down center armrest, regardless of body type. The Brougham Cloth Trim option was a slightly altered version of the previous year's SL offering.

A major development in the air conditioning system was released in response to other manufacturers' offerings. Dubbed Automatic Climate Control (later called Automatic Temperature Control), the system used a thermostatic-regulated control head to switch between the air conditioner and heater, as well as control blower speed, to maintain consistent interior temperatures when the system was on. Most buyers, as usual, opted for air conditioning.

A novel accessory innovation, the Rear Lamp Monitor, took advantage of another new technological development, fiber optics. Individual translucent plastic rods were installed in the taillight housings, so that the ends could be exposed to each of the signal bulbs. On the

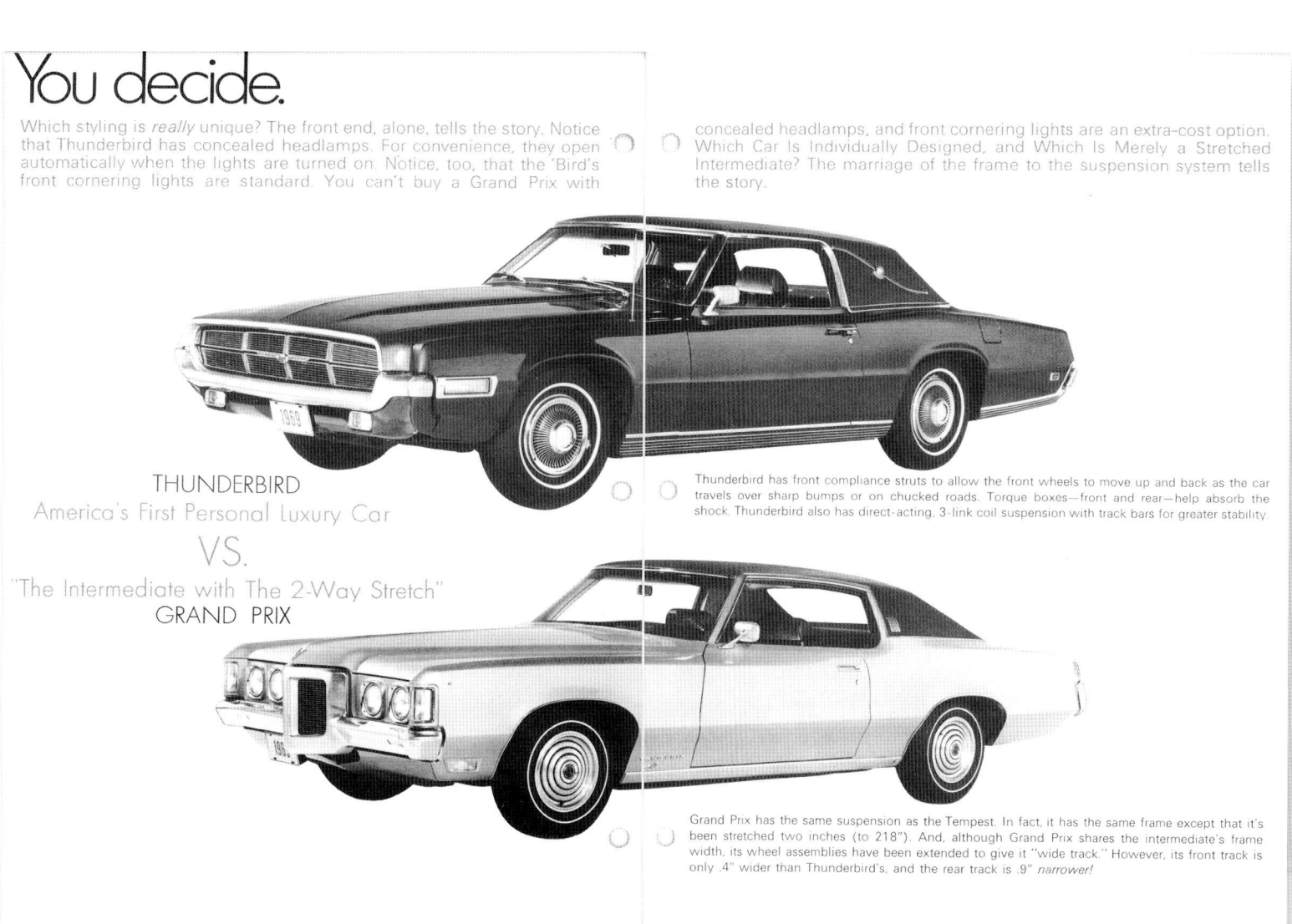

Lincoln finally had its own Thunderbird with the Mark III. Adapted from the 4-door Landau chassis, it provided a high-end alternative to the T-Bird. Alan H. Tast collection

rear package tray, a housing was mounted which faced forward and contained the other end of the rods, which were bundled together as they passed through the trunk. When the brakes or turn signals were activated, light from the light bulbs was transmitted from the exposed end of the rod to the other exposed end in the monitor housing. If the bulb was burned out, the corresponding end in the monitor would be dark. The driver was supposed to see this in the rearview mirror. Not many were installed, and the option was dropped at the end of the 1969 model year. Even harder to find today is the matching set of luggage that was available through dealers.

Public introduction of the 1968 line took place on September 22, 1967. For the first time, Ford expanded Thunderbird production to two assembly plants, refurbishing its eastern Los Angeles facility, known as Pico Rivera, to share the burden with Wixom. Yet a company-wide strike shut down production almost immediately. Once Ford and the UAW had come to terms, they accelerated output to make up the lost time. But refinements in the car and a strong showing by the other personal luxury makes meant fewer Thunderbirds for 1968. Output declined to 64,931.

Like in past eras, money was held back for a more-thorough facelift for the third year of the run. The exterior changes for 1969 included a new rear valance with separate turn signal assemblies and a concealed backup light in the center of a charcoal gray-painted panel accented with chrome-plated, raised ribs and the Thunderbird name in individual letters. The grille was reworked, with two rows of chrome-framed panels containing horizontal chromed ribs. The Thunderbird emblem, with aqua-colored plastic inserts for the wings and body, was centered over the two rows. The lower front valance housed restyled turn signal indicators, while side markers also incorporated cornering lights. The rear marker light was changed to a small rectangle with a chrome-plated Thunderbird emblem. The lower body trim on the rocker panels and bottom of the rear quarters was also changed to mimic the ribbed grille texture with charcoal gray recesses, and an added aluminum trim spear running from behind the front wheel cutout back around the rear bumper reveal.

The interior was relatively unchanged with the exception of fabrics and patterns. Now 9 colors were available in combination with additional selections between bench versus bucket seats, and the usual cloth/vinyl/leather covers, for a total of 29 choices. Two-doors offered unique, burgundy leather bucket seats. All models featured front-seat headrests/restraints, as required by federal law. Bucket seat orders were down to 16,769, representing only 34 percent of the 1969 T-Birds.

Harking back to 1966, stylists distinguished the Landau from the two-door hardtop with a blind-quarter roof. As on the 1966 Town version, window corners were rounded off. The roof line created a formal look and added $140 to the base hardtop's price of $4,807. For the hardtop, sales brochures originally showed a Thunderbird script on the lower front of the C-pillar. In production form, the roof Bird with background surround was reused. Both the hardtop and Landau could be ordered with vinyl roofs, but only the Landau got the alligator-grain pattern.

New options included a pair of turn signal light pods that mounted on the outboard sides of the rear windows. Called High Brake Lights, these could be considered the precursor of today's shelf-mounted third brake light. Also new for keeping the rear windows clear on cold, frosty mornings was an electrically heated grid of wires glued to the glass. On the performance side, the innovation of the year was an anti-lock brake system for the rear axle called "Sure-Track."

But the one option that everyone noticed was another throwback to the T-Bird's history—a steel-paneled sunroof, this time motorized. American Sunroof Company (ASC) again provided the parts to modify and install the roof assembly, not only for the T-Bird, but also for the Cougar. Marketing played up the "sunroof door" to the hilt in advertising and prominently featured it in the sales brochure. To simplify production, only the Pico Rivera plant installed sunroofs.

Overall, 1969 wasn't a better year than 1968. Sales continued to go backward, with overall production backsliding 15,659 units to end up at 49,272. The four-door Landau accounted for 15,650 cars, making it again the second favorite behind the 27,664 two-door Landaus. Hardtops fell far short of five-figure sales, at 5,913 cars. In the second year of bi-plant assembly operations, the Wixom plant outdid Pico Rivera by a rate of 40,571 units to 8,701.

The decade did not end as well as marketing had hoped—yet for all the changes, the Thunderbird retained its one constant quality: unique style. Its unique style was about to change again.

CHAPTER SIX

1970–1971
The Beak Goes On

Originally used in 1969 and dropped for 1970, the 1971 Landau brought back the blind-quarter roof, like this Goldenrod and Brown example.

(above) Even though the rear deck lid hinted at the twin pontoon theme used since the 1950s, taillights for 1970–1971 had more in common with Pontiac's inverted "U" thanks to Bunkie Knudsen's influence.

(opposite) The nose panel provided a place for the 'Bird emblem in 1970–1971.

Chevrolet's entry into the personal luxury market was the 1970 Monte Carlo, which was available with a range of engines from the small-block 350 to the monster 454-ci SS version shown here. John Lee

The story of the 1970–1971 Thunderbird is intertwined in corporate politics as much as it is in the normal development of an automobile. Why did the extension of the fifth generation of the Thunderbird turn out like it did? You can thank (or blame) one person: Semon E. "Bunkie" Knudsen. A fixture at General Motors for decades, Knudsen was lured to Ford by Henry II in February 1968—just as the 1970 and 1971 Thunderbirds were in the design stage.

Knudsen became president and chief operating officer, and gained a seat on Ford Motor Company's board of directors. His resume included an engineering degree from MIT, general manager of Detroit Diesel, head of Pontiac, and general manager of Chevrolet. He was instrumental in expanding Chevy's Super Sport program and in developing the Corvette Stingray. From there, he became General Motors' executive vice president, before accepting Henry II's offer.

One of Knudsen's first moves was to bring Larry Shinoda over from GM. Shinoda worked for Ford from 1954 through 1956, before Harley Earl hired him to work at the GM Design Center. Shinoda gained prominence with his work on the 1959 Chevrolet, then caught Bunkie's eye with his contribution to the 1960–1961 Pontiacs during 1958. He

98　　　**Chapter Six**

worked on the Sting Ray concept racer of the late 1950s, and then the Corvette Stingray for 1963 and the Z-28 Camaro in 1967.

At Ford, Shinoda jumped right in, shaping the 1969 Boss 302 and Boss 429 Mustangs. When he finished that project, he was ready to contribute to other Ford products. Candidates for 1970 overhaul included the Thunderbird and, at the same time, the Fairlane/Torino. Yet Ford had just spent big dollars developing the new Maverick and Comet. The design budget for Thunderbird and Torino was limited to body shell updates to make them appear more aerodynamic. For Torino, this was a functional change, since Knudsen saw it as Ford's NASCAR super-speedway standard-bearer. Carrying its look over to the Thunderbird advanced one of Bunkie's design philosophies: you can sell a young man's car to an old man, but not the other way around.

For the two-door car, which would come to be known as the "SportsRoof," Knudsen and Shinoda drew inspiration from a pair of T-Bird show cars from 1968–1969, called Saturn I and Saturn II. Both show cars were similar, with fastback-like roofs, wide-mouth grilles like the 1967–1969 T-Birds, and minimal trim. The hood was pulled up and over the cowl in order to conceal the windshield wipers. Sides received more sculpturing over the top of the rear quarters.

For the GM transplants, another source of inspiration was fresh in their pasts. The most controversial parts of the production design looked to many like direct knock-offs of Pontiac trademarks. To break away from the vacuum-cleaner front, a very pronounced "beak" was grafted to the front header panel. Inside this proboscis, a series of extruded and formed aluminum bars went across the width of the center grille. Paired headlights, left

The 1970–1971 Sportsroof styling was intended to make Thunderbird more appealing to performance-minded buyers.

(above) The last of the four-door T-Birds carried over most of the bodywork of previous versions from the cowl back.

(right) The 1971 four-doors were the only models to have a high-back split front bench seat.

open, were recessed into the outboard ends. At the rear, full-width taillights returned, but this time the lenses turned down at the ends, creating an inverted "U" shape. Both of these features could be directly traced to late 1960s production Ponchos. The pointed nose was used on virtually every model from the Firebird to the GTO, albeit with a split grille. How did the new and improved Thunderbird compare with its predecessor? While wheelbases and powertrains didn't change from 1969, the body's proportions obviously did. The overall length of the two-door and four-door models was stretched nearly six inches, with the two-door now staking out 212.5 inches from front to back and the four-door stretched 215.5 inches. Side to side, the two-door was the fatter of the two at 78 inches compared to 77.4 inches for the four-slammer. Weight increased only six pounds for the hardtop, to 4,354 pounds, and four for the two-door Landau, to 4,464 pounds. The four-door Landau tipped the scales at 4,630 pounds.

Because most of the budget went to the SportsRoof, the four-door Landau carried over the 1969's body shell with the new front clip. The four-door didn't have as high a priority for a full-blown makeover. In fact, another cost-cutting decision was to not have a formal-roof Landau. Unlike the previous year, the base and Landau two-doors would share the same body—Knudsen believed that all two-doors needed a sporty image. The Landau also went without an S-bar or other distinctive ornamentation. Only the teak-appliqué interior and Cayman vinyl roof separated the Landau from the base hardtop. Buyers could also opt for moldings along the mid-body feature line. Depending on other features, these body side moldings were either filled with a black vinyl strip or left plain.

Interior refinements were limited. The 1969 dash was reused, as was the console for cars ordered with bucket seats. Door panels were changed in the area above the armrests. The T-Bird used the Mustang's new Rim-Blow tri-spoked steering wheel, but with no suspended horn ring or horn pad on the spokes. Instead, the inside of the rim could be depressed anywhere on its circumference to energize the two-tone horns. Once again, the high-level brake lights were offered as an option.

A new federal law for 1970 required passenger cars to have the ignition switch located on the steering column, to lock the steering wheel and transmission gear selector in place. The switch also had to be connected to a buzzer that sounded if the key was left in the ignition. The clumsy shoulder belt introduced in 1967 was revised so that it connected to the lap belt. Even the glove-box lock had to be engineered so that it would remain closed in a collision. Exhaust emission controls were also expanding beyond California to the rest of the nation. The 1970 cars used a vacuum-switch linking the thermostat housing to the distributor. This mechanism advanced or retarded spark in relation to engine temperature.

The sportiest-looking models were those with the Fiera, or Special Brougham, package, also offered in 1971. This option featured amber driving lights in the grille just inboard of the headlight assemblies, as well as full wheel covers painted to match the body. To give the cockpit a unique feel, the Special Brougham package provided high-back bucket seats adapted from the Mustang, with Hopsack cloth inserts and an embroidered Thunderbird emblem. With conventional and high-back versions available, customers ordered bucket seats 23,883 times, in just under half of 1970 Thunderbirds.

Released in September 1969, the new Thunderbird drew mixed reactions. It may have also contributed to Knudsen losing his job at Ford; he was fired on September 11, 1969. Bunkie and Henry II didn't see eye to eye on everything, and Bunkie's ambition to make changes plus push performance didn't sit well with his boss. There was also animosity between Knudsen and the upwardly aspiring Lee Iacocca. According to the 1969 Annual Report, a "major realignment" was made in the wake of Knudsen's departure, creating three distinct operating groups: Ford North American Automotive Operations, headed by Iacocca as president, Ford International Automotive Operations, and Ford Nonautomotive Operations. Shinoda left Ford too, after completing work on the 1971–1973 Mustang, and began his own industrial design firm.

Sales for 1970 appeared to be going in the right direction, rising to 50,346 units and bettering the previous year's sales by 1,092 units. Buyers paid base prices of $4,961 for the hardtop, $5,104 for the Landau, and $5,182 for the four-door—a modest increase of around $150 over the 1969s. Yet insurance companies were putting the squeeze on buyers, in response to abnormally high claims for front-end repair. The new nose stuck out farther than on any other Ford product, short of the Mercury Cyclone. And the grille, bumper, and upper header panel were not cheap to replace.

Because of expenses elsewhere, such as on Mustang and the new Pinto, Ford slated minimal updates for the 1971 Thunderbird. The only drastic change was the return of the formal blind-quarter roof for the Landau. Iacocca and Ford's head of styling, Gene Bordinat, saw this as a break from Knudsen's sports philosophy for a luxury car and as way to reestablish the conservative lines they felt middle-aged buyers wanted. The base hardtop could be ordered with a vinyl roof, even on cars with a sunroof.

Body side moldings could now be color-keyed to the body, as well as the wheel covers, when buyers opted for the Exterior Appearance Group or Special Brougham Option. The Exterior Appearance Group also gave owners body-colored grille panels and stone shields, along with bright metal trim along the upper edges of the wheel arches. Front and rear bumper guards with vinyl inserts could also be installed.

Under the hood, engineers fitted charcoal canisters to trap gas fumes, according to federal law. The T-Bird kept its four-barrel 429 engine, and its 10.5:1 compression ratio—unlike GM, which detuned its engines to reduce horsepower and burn cheaper, lower-octane gas. The lone performance options for 1971 were a heavy-duty suspension upgrade, with heavier springs and stiffer shock absorbers, and the Traction-Lok rear axle, with either the standard 2.80:1 or optional 3.00:1 drive ratio.

A major revision inside, available only in the four-door with the Brougham Interior Option group, was an optional high-back split bench seat with individual armrests. The option gave the Thunderbird buyer high and low versions of both bucket and bench seats. The high-back individual bucket seats were again available as part of the Special Brougham package, which

Personal luxury cars were more prone to designers' excesses. The 1971 Buick Riviera made a radical styling move with its boattail rear.
Alan H. Tast collection

also included the Rim-Blow steering wheel and pull straps on the doors. Switches for the 6-way power seat, door locks, windows, and the remote control mirror joystick filled the forward, upper driver's door armrest in the "Driver's Control Console."

Adding to the interior package choices was the Turnpike Convenience Group, combining a new two-spoke steering wheel with fingertip speed (cruise) controls, and a reclining passenger seat. Michelin steel-belted narrow-band whitewall tires rounded out the package. Standard seating was a vinyl-sheathed low-back bench seat with adjustable headrests.

Salesmen must have had a tough year making commissions and quotas off of the 1971 Thunderbird. For the post-classic era, it was the lowest-selling edition with exception of the post-Millennium two-seaters. Not helping Thunderbird's appeal was an increase in base prices, with the no-frills base hardtop running $5,295. The formal-roof Landau went up $334 to start at $5,438, and the four-door Landau was the priciest at $5,516. Final production for the year was only 36,055 cars.

The sixth generation Thunderbird became the pawn in a Ford management chess game. If Knudsen would have had more time to pursue a powerful, youthful design, he might have restored Thunderbird to its sporting roots, or pushed it beyond them. Yet the market itself was retreating from that realm, with reduced power and emissions. As it was, the next generation would reflect Iacocca's view of what a Thunderbird should be: Big.

CHAPTER SEVEN

1972–1976
Luxury Land Yacht

Copper Fire, one of the Glamour Paint options for 1972, also included color-keyed wheel covers, tooled silver Landau bars, and pinstripes.

(right) The front-end styling for 1972 was a refinement of 1971's, with the nose and grille pulled back. The front bumper's svelte appearance only lasted one year.

(opposite) The 1972 interiors were somewhat restrained with a more conventional dash layout and cut-pile carpet. The sunroof was a $505 option.

The 1973–1976 models shared the same front end with 5-mile-per-hour bumpers and separated headlights. Among the rare color combinations for 1975 was the Copper Edition with a Polar White body, Copper vinyl roof, and pinstripes.

Born a trim and nimble two-seat personal luxury car, the Thunderbird had been changing, growing longer and heavier with age. It also saw its market share decline as others made a bid for affluent buyers, including the Lincoln Mark III, which it spawned. The platform introduced for 1967 and given a facelift for 1970 was getting long in the tooth. With sales plummeting, the underlying design could not survive another two- to three-year cycle with only minor refinements.

The seventh generation car was like a favorite uncle approaching middle age. It grew in girth and became more comfortable, more sedate. It didn't grow because it wanted to, but because it had to. Cars like the front-wheel-drive Cadillac El Dorado and Oldsmobile Toronado, along with rear-wheel-drive variant Buick Riviera, were on the same plane (if not slightly above) the T-Bird's level, while intermediate makeovers, Pontiac's Grand Prix and Chevrolet's Monte Carlo, added pressure from the bottom end of the scale.

Buyers of personal luxury cars were looking for a softer ride with less emphasis on performance and more on creature comfort. To achieve this, manufacturers extended wheelbases, added room to the interior and padding to the seats, and put more convenience gadgets at drivers' fingertips. If the extra space and creature comforts added weight, hurt aerodynamics, and reduced gas mileage, no one cared. With U.S. prices averaging around 30 cents a gallon for premium, people were willing to spend another couple of dollars to tank up and hit the interstate at 75 miles per hour.

Designers and engineers had a fairly clear assignment for the new Thunderbird and sister Mark IV in the summer of 1969. They were to develop a platform that could be used for up to five years, provide it with the biggest engine Ford had available, and load it down with as many convenience-driven features as possible. There was one departure from the size-is-no-object formula: They would not design a four-door model. The public had made clear over the previous five years that it had little interest in another set of doors. For the first time since 1957, Ford would offer only one body style—no blind-quarter or fastback roof deviants, no drop-tops—just a single two-door hardtop coupe. A vinyl roof would be the major feature distinguishing higher-end from base models.

Bunkie Knudsen and Larry Shinoda were still with Ford during the early design phases. Early concepts for the new Thunderbird carried forward the pointed-nose grille, but in subdued fashion. The two-light headlight pods were retained, as

(below) The 1975 Copper Edition was available in copper-colored velour cloth or leather. It was the unofficial 20th anniversary car for Thunderbird.

(bottom) The Thunderbird name was spelled out on the nose pane of 1973–1976 models.

Advertising for 1975 called attention to 20th anniversary models in copper (shown) and silver. Alan H. Tast collection

was the full-width taillight panel with a large Thunderbird emblem in the center. The major departure from the past would be the long hood and short rear-deck concept—a trend that caught fire first with the Mustang and Cougar.

Because Thunderbird's target market was a solidly middle-aged, conservative group, no hip- or mod-influenced colors or trims were given consideration. Aircraft-inspired styling gave way to simplicity. The new instrument panel featured a row of "idiot" lights across the top of a squared-off opening containing the speedometer, gear selector indicator, light and wiper controls, and the heater control panel. Power window switches were retained on the forward part of the driver's door armrest. The steering wheel could be had in two-spoke form or the three-spoke "Rim-Blow" option. Wood-tone appliqués were limited to rectangular inserts in the upper door panel, and trim/switch panels on the armrest and dash. Michelin radial tires as standard equipment became a selling feature on the 1972. Providing a long list of profit-producing options was also a basic element in the Thunderbird formula for success.

The Torino-based Elite was considered a baby Thunderbird with its plethora of luxury appointments. The Elite was a precursor for the 1977–1979 T-Bird. Alan H. Tast

Seating choices for the base offering were limited to a split-bench seat in Lamont Cloth and Vinyl until early in 1972, when a flight-bench seat became standard; through a mid-year change, the split bench became an option. Leather was available on the split bench at additional cost. One option that wasn't as popular was high-back bucket seats shod in Hopsack cloth. Available only with a center console, only 8,036 cars (13.9 percent) were equipped this way. Seat colors included black, dark blue, dark red, ginger, dark green, and tobacco; one ginger/tobacco combination; and four combinations of white seats with different color appointments.

Thunderbird became nearly as large as the full-size Ford sedans, including the LTD. The overall length of the 1972 version was 17 feet, 10 inches. The car's width expanded by almost three inches from its predecessor to 79.3, or almost 10 inches more than the 1955 two-seater. Its height stayed between the previous year's body styles at 52.1 inches, or about half an inch shorter than the 4-door and Landau models, but an inch and a half taller than the SportsRoof hardtop. Between the wheels, it also stretched its legs by almost half a foot over the fifth generation two-doors, to 120.4 inches—slightly over 10 feet.

Lincoln's Mark IV shared the Thunderbird platform and production line. Alan H. Tast collection

Sometime between August 1971 and January 1972, Ford dropped the new, smaller engine from a 400-ci V-8, which was originally listed as the standard T-Bird engine for 1972, in favor of the more powerful 429. The 400-ci engine was deemed too small for the car. The 429 was still larger than any standard or optional engine previously available in the Thunderbird with the exception of the optional 430 offered in 1959 and 1960. Although the Thunderbird was less of a muscle car and more of a land yacht, it relied on mega-cubic inches and high compression for motivation.

General Motors detuned their cars in 1971 by lowering compression ratios. They also advertised lower horsepower ratings by measuring output with all accessories installed. Ford had to follow suit in 1972, decreasing compression from 10.5:1 to 8.5:1, with an apparent decrease in horsepower from 360 to 212 at 4,400 rpm. Torque readings likewise dropped from 480 to 327 foot-pounds at 2,600 rpm. In reality, the decrease in power was not as dramatic as stated, because the new number was net rather than gross horsepower. The old numbers were overstated because they were gathered from an unburdened engine. To counter the drop in power (part real, part perceived), by mid-year Ford decided to offer the Lincoln 460, which was standard in the Mark IV, as an optional engine. The 460 produced 12 more horsepower and 11 more foot-pounds of torque than the standard 429.

Introduced on September 24, 1971, along with a newly designed Torino/Montego intermediate line, the Thunderbird and Mark IV began their run against GM's year-old personal luxury designs, including the boldly styled Buick "boat-tail" Riviera. Critics' initial reviews were not overly flattering. Commentators made light of the fact that the T-Bird had grown bloated to appease the ever-softening middle class buyer. Yet, over 57,000 people put their names on sales contracts for them, which was better than 1971's tally.

Options could send the Thunderbird's base price of $5,293 up to over $8,500 for a fully loaded car. The typical Thunderbird was sold with a vinyl roof and Landau bars—less than 2 percent had a plain metal top. The typical Landau had woodgrain inserts in the S-bars, while the upscale Glamour Paint Option with vinyl roof came with tooled silver inserts. The Glamour Paint Option, which was limited to eight highly metallic "Fire" colors, not only had an exclusive set of landau bars, but it also included color-keyed wheel covers, dual body side and hood paint pinstriping. All together, there were 23 exterior colors available, including 8 metallics and the aforementioned "Fire" metallics. Air conditioning was so popular that only about 536 cars were built without it. Buyers went with power seats in 44,784 examples.

One very special car was produced in 1972. Ford determined that it would produce the one millionth Thunderbird during mid- to late June. With lobbying from influential members of the Classic Thunderbird Club International, the company decided to loan the car for a year to the club's "Best of Show" winner at its 1972 national convention in Los Angeles. The car featured a special gold exterior paint treatment with white bodyside moldings, vinyl roof, and interior. The landau bars displayed a unique "One Millionth T-Bird" logo, with driver-side profiles of both a 1955 and 1972 T-Bird. A month before the show on June 22, 1972, Pico Rivera assembled the car, promoted it, then put it in the convention hotel's show field. George Watts, who also held title to the first production Thunderbird, bought the one-millionth car following the one-year loan. By the late 1980s, Bob Peterson, another Thunderbird aficionado, bought the car.

Final model-year production for 1972 was 57,814—60 percent better than 1971's performance. The next year would do even better.

In the second year of the cycle, safety upgrades added to the car's bulk. Federal law required that by 1973, front bumpers had to withstand a 5 mile-per-hour impact without damage. To do this, engineers developed a boxier bumper that projected beyond the body's sheet metal, concealing a pair of large shock absorbers. The 1973 car's length grew only 2.9 inches because the bumper wrapped around the turn signal extensions to keep it close

to the 1972's overall dimensions. Because of the new bumper structure, cutouts for the air intakes used on the 1972 were gone.

Also on the outside, designers reworked the header panel to separate the headlights into individual bezels. The 1973 used a crosshatch grille below the word "Thunderbird," which was spelled out in block letters for the first time since 1964. The Thunderbird emblem appeared on the rear taillight lens, as well as on the new-to-Thunderbird hood ornament. The other major change was deletion of the S-bar to make room for an optional trapezoidal-shaped opera window. The window became standard on the 1974 car. Few buyers purchased T-Birds with the plain metal roof (roughly 220 cars), no air conditioning (524 cars), and no power windows (698 cars).

Color choices changed somewhat, but there were still 23 to select from. Fifteen metallics, including eight Glamour/Fire hues, spiced up the list. On the interior side, six solid colors and four white options trimmed with color-keyed appointments were available for the standard split-bench seat. While cloth/vinyl upholstery was standard for the split-bench seat, an optional all-vinyl or leather seat surface was available. High-back bucket seats were also on the dealer's list of upgrades, but even fewer takers were found than in the previous year. They were dropped for 1974.

Since little changed for the year, accountants must have been happy that sales increased to 87,269 units. The price of the car changed, though, to $5,577 for the base model; this was an increase of $284 from 1972. In March 1973, President Nixon froze prices by executive order to stem inflation, which was at 8.5 percent per year and increasing. With increased sales for 1973, prognosticators at the "Glass House" must have been confident that 1974 would be more of the same. Global events would prove otherwise.

The OPEC (Organization of Petroleum Exporting Countries) oil embargo, from October 1973 to March 1974, sent gas prices skyward from about 30 cents to $1.20 per gallon. Suddenly cars with poor fuel economy were unpopular and expensive to operate. Gas rationing hurt the same cars more, because service station owners responded to a plea from President Nixon and began limiting sales to 10 gallons per customer. Suddenly that 22.5-gallon tank was less than half as useful.

What changed for 1974? Bucket seats and a center console dropped from the option list, thus creating the first T-Bird since 1957 to offer only a bench seat. The instrument panel was now color-keyed. Added safety features like the 5 mile-per-hour collision-safe rear bumper increased the car's weight by almost 50 pounds and its length to 225 inches overall, partially because front bumper guards were now standard equipment. This would make it the largest passenger car in Ford Division history for virtually every dimension. Taillights were redesigned as a multi-segment panel with a center back-up light. The vinyl top was now standard equipment, along with the opera windows, power windows, and air conditioning. Under the hood, the 460 was the only engine available, albeit at a detuned 218 horsepower at 4,400 rpm and 355 foot-pounds of torque at 600 rpm with now-standard electronic ignition. To help stem the weight gain, a space-saver spare was offered for the first time.

In an effort to bolster sagging sales, new option packages were developed for release in mid–production. The Burgundy Luxury

(opposite) By 1974, the rear bumpers were required to meet the same impact standards as the front and added to the car's bulk, such as on this Dark Brown Metallic 1976 model.

(below) Spring-loaded hood ornaments with an oval surround were introduced on T-Birds in 1973 and continued to adorn front ends through 1976.

Group was quickly followed by the "Gold and White Luxury Group." These would be the first of several similar packages offered over the next few years. These packages highlighted specific color/trim combinations, augmented with luxury items such as upgraded wheel treatment and trunk trim. (The "Gold and White Luxury Group" of 1974 was different from and less dramatic than the "Gold and Cream" edition of 1976.)

The base price for a Thunderbird escalated by $1,677, a whopping 22.8 percent! The increase was somewhat mitigated in that $952 worth of options were now standard. Only 58,443 Thunderbirds rolled out of Wixom and Pico Rivera, down 28,826 in one year. Production ended for the 1974s at about the same time that President Nixon addressed the nation on August 8 to announce he was resigning from the Presidency.

The nation was not in an upbeat mood, and neither was Ford Motor Company. Dwindling sales and losses in market share created a panicked atmosphere in the company. Imports of Japanese and European fuel-efficient compacts compounded the problem of a lagging economy, surging inflation, and rejection of the norm rigeur. Rather than continue to

The last 1976 Thunderbird, a painted Bright Gold Metallic, is displayed after it rolled off the final acceptance line at Wixom on July 9, 1976. Alan H. Tast collection

invest in development of established lines, which now were at a competitive disadvantage due to poor fuel economy and rising costs, executives decided to focus resources toward new lines of downsized cars. This in effect froze funds for face-lifting the Thunderbird, and until a new generation could be ready for production in the summer of 1976, only colors and options would change. Mandatory changes for 1975 included a catalytic converter. As a result, the car again gained 68 pounds to top out at 4,893 pounds in standard trim. It was the heaviest T-Bird ever produced.

Several interesting and now desirable options came to fruition for 1975. Four-wheel disc brakes became available for the first time on a production Ford. Perhaps the most interesting technological innovation was an electrically heated windshield and rear window. Driven by a separate 24-volt/70-amp alternator, a thin layer of metallic film sandwiched between the two layers of glass in the windshield created a heated surface that would melt ice and snow when switched on. The option was not popular due to its cost, and replacing the special windshield was very expensive.

One bright note for the Thunderbird was that it was the nameplate's 20th Anniversary. Ford played this up in its sales literature and even developed a few new luxury groups. The Copper and Silver Luxury Groups originally provided to celebrate the "china" anniversary were followed by the Jade Luxury Group. The Copper edition had copper trim inside and out with either Copper Fire or Polar White paint. You could only get the silver edition with a silver exterior, but you could have either a red or silver interior. The Jade group was truly a mix and match. The exterior could be Polar White or Jade with either a white or green vinyl top, and the interior could be Jade or Jade and White. Upgrades in wheels and trunk lining were also included.

Prices for the base model increased by $480 for 1975, which didn't help sales. Production again dropped, to 42,685 cars, continuing the backslide from 1974. Perhaps another factor behind the decline was the upscale Torino, introduced in 1974. This car was called the Elite. Many would refer to it as a "baby Thunderbird" because it was appointed as well as a T-Bird or a well-equipped Mercury Cougar. Its advantages over the T-Bird were less weight, a smaller engine, and better gas mileage.

The 1976 model year brought no outstanding changes for the T-Bird. Perhaps the biggest change was a Quadraphonic Stereo sound system. Luxury groups were given new colors of Bordeaux (a dark burgundy), Lipstick (bright red), and at the highest end, the Crème and Gold two-tone. Of the three, the Crème and Gold Edition is perhaps the best known since it was the most unique. It featured a special gold-anodized dash trim, and gold pinstriping to separate the gold-painted body side from the crème-colored hood and front roof half. An attractive set of chromed aluminum road wheels also set off the exterior, while on the inside a gold velour or leather upholstery and deep, cut-pile carpeting topped off the package.

Sales for 1976 increased as Ford made known that this would be the last year for the Big Bird. Production rebounded to 52,935 units, and on July 9, 1976, just five days after the nation celebrated its bicentennial, the last of the large Thunderbirds, a painted Bright Gold Metallic, was driven through the final inspection station at the Wixom plant.

CHAPTER EIGHT

1977–1979
Trim & Proper

The 1977 and 1978 Thunderbirds were virtually identical. The Diamond Jubilee edition was developed to celebrate Ford's 75th anniversary in 1978. Diamond Blue Metallic was the most popular color, but it was also available in Ember Metallic and in Polar White with Diamond Blue or Ember vinyl roof and interior trim.

(right) The late 1970s was a time of downsizing. T-Birds used smaller, lighter engines such as the 351M with an aluminum air-cleaner assembly, to increase fuel economy and lower emissions.

(opposite) The Diamond Jubilee was identified by a thickly padded vinyl roof that covered the C-pillar window, and silk-screened B-pillar windows.

After years of only dreaming about six digit sales figures, Ford finally figured out how to develop and market a Thunderbird for the masses. The 1977 version, smaller and cheaper than its predecessor, was the first Thunderbird to sell over 100,000 units. Over the following two model years, eighth generation production would surpass the quarter-million mark—more sales than the first 16 years combined. The success of the 1977–1979 Thunderbird could be used by college economics and marketing professors as a case study in how trading on the value of an established product can help to spur sales.

The smaller Thunderbird owed its success in part to world events. Following the OPEC crisis, gas prices surged and for the first time since World War II, U.S. car buyers paid attention to how many miles their vehicle could travel on each gallon. At the same time, the government stepped in to mitigate the crisis. In 1975, it established Corporate Average Fuel Economy (CAFE) standards, under which auto makers would have to meet rising fuel efficiency benchmarks. Other forces also pressured U.S. auto makers, including small, economical Japanese imports.

The Thunderbird hit its biggest, heaviest, most glutinous state, when the market changed course and rewarded smaller, inexpensive vehicles with modest appetites. The public shunned the 5,000-pound monsters rolling out of Wixom and Pico Rivera with their 460-ci engines in favor of relatively more economical cars like the Elite, Monte Carlo, and Chrysler Cordoba. Mid-size personal luxury was suddenly "in." Luckily, Ford had already begun planning for a new platform to replace the Torino and Montego lines. The replacements, slated for release during the 1977 model year, were set up to provide a large amount of flexibility in packaging and production. Management decided to make Thunderbird the top-of-the-line version of the mid-size car.

The new T-Bird used a 114-inch wheelbase (just one inch longer than the 1958–1966 models), pulling the front and rear axles 6.4 inches closer together. Overall length was compressed 10.7 inches from 1976, to 215.5 inches, while width dropped 1 1/2 inches to 78.5 inches. Designers and engineers whittled away at every component they could to reduce weight, shaving 900 pounds from the car for a base model weight of 3,907 pounds—a 20.8 percent loss.

Under the hood, designers installed the 302-ci Windsor engine, with a two-barrel carburetor, single exhaust, and catalytic converter. Strangely enough, Californians could only get the 351 Modified, a refined version of the 351 Cleveland mill, offered as an option in the other 49 states. It made 12 more horses and 6 more ft-lbs of torque than the 351 Windsor. The biggest displacement available was 400-ci, breaking the tradition of giving the Thunderbird Ford's largest engine. For 1977 this honor went to the LTD, with the 460-ci Police Interceptor.

To distinguish three car lines, Ford stylists developed different roof, taillight, and front-end treatments. The LTD II was the more traditional, rounder, full-size Ford with a variety of body types. The Cougar line included sister cars to the Thunderbird and the LTD II. The

(above) To carry forward what the Diamond Jubilee started, the Heritage edition was the top T-Bird for 1979, such as this unique maroon example.

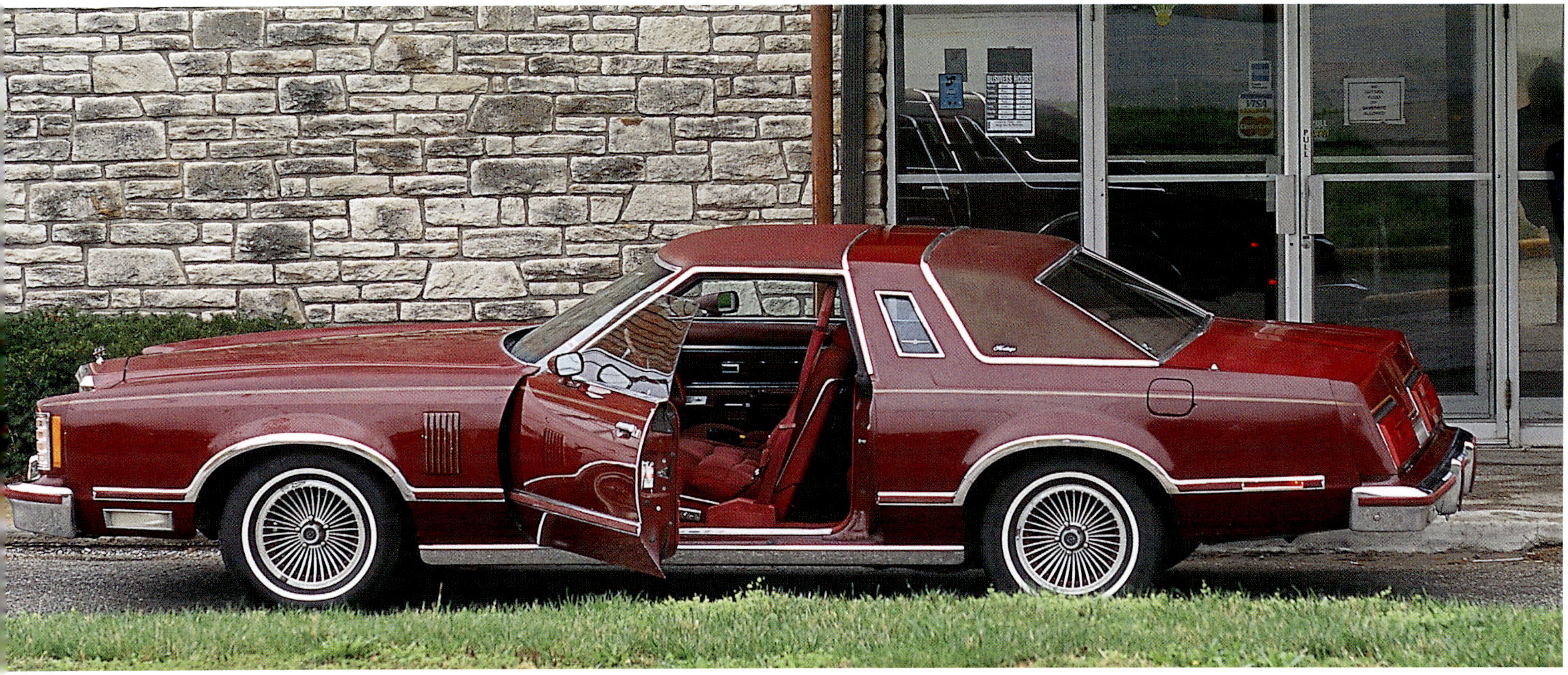

(below) Heritage's rear side window was covered and an emblem was installed to distinguish it from other 1979 T-Birds.

(above) American Custom Coachworks of Beverly Hills built two-seat custom versions of the 1977 and 1978 T-Birds, and reworked the top to retain the rear seats in 1979. They were sold through Ford dealers. Approximately 200 were built for 1979.

(right) Ford called its factory-built open variant for 1978 1/2–1979 the T-Roof Convertible. Separate taillights and a center back-up light distinguish the 1979 models from 1977-1978s.

120 Chapter Eight

The 1979 Cougar XR-7 was Mercury's twin to the Thunderbird. Additional models of the Cougar, including a four-door sedan and a station wagon, were more like the LTD II. Alan H. Tast collection

T-Bird's true sister was the Cougar XR7. The XR7, and later the base Cougar, would remain closely tied with the Thunderbird through 1997.

The T-Bird was the most radical of the three. Designers raked the B-pillar forward, gave it a small window, and then placed a larger window between it and the C-pillar. A brushed stainless-steel tiara on the Town Landau, introduced mid-year, further emphasized this roof-window treatment.

Ford introduced its new line over the first weekend of October 1976, making Thunderbird the featured car. A total of 16 exterior colors and 12 matching or contrasting vinyl roofs, including mid-year returns of Lipstick Red and Dark Jade Metallic packages, were available. Rose Glow Metallic was unique to T-Bird. Interior choices included 6 solid colors, 6 two-tones featuring white appointments, and one combination of white with saddle appointments. Buyers could replace standard cloth-and-vinyl bench seats up front with eight other choices, starting with all-vinyl bench or bucket seats, or a vinyl and two-tone

The Diamond Jubilee Edition was featured in an advertisement in 1978. Alan H. Tast collection

houndstooth-pattern cloth bucket seat. Another step up from the base selections was the Interior Décor Group, featuring special appointments and fabrics. Leather was available with a split-bench seat.

One way Ford made the 1977 T-Bird cheaper than the 1976 was by removing standard features—like better seats, power windows, vinyl roof, color-keyed seatbelts, air conditioning, bumper guards, rub strips, outside passenger side remote mirror and body side moldings—and making them options. The new car offered buyers at least 44 optional items, including the once-desirable 8-track stereo with quadraphonic sound. An extended-range 27.5-gallon fuel tank came standard on the Town Landau, and was optional for other T-Birds. Less than half of new owners ordered power windows, power driver's seat, and tilt steering column, while most still went for the vinyl top, and all but a small percentage ordered air conditioning.

(above left) While most Heritage editions for 1979 were either blue or maroon, a few were built in Polar White with powder blue rub strips, triple-band pinstripes, turbine wheels, and grille.

(above) The 1979 Heritage featured plush 36-ounce cut-pile carpeting, leather-wrapped steering wheel and dash pad, velour-covered seats, and the Sports Instrumentation Group.

(left) This Light Medium Blue 1979 Heritage was almost double the cost of a base T-Bird at $10,687 versus $5,877 for a stripped down model.

Advertising across the range of Ford mid-size products gave consumers a chance to compare the top-of-the-line T-Bird with its cousin, the LTD II, and its stablemate, the Granada.
Alan H. Tast collection

The Town Landau version, available only once before, in 1966, provided a buyer with over 190 pounds' worth of added goodies for $2,927 over the base price of $5,063. Numerous touches distinguished the model, including a brushed stainless-steel tiara, center side windows with the model designation silk-screened onto the glass, color-coordinated crystal hood ornament, dual sport mirrors, cast-aluminum turbine wheels, and pinstriping in a contrasting color. The Town Landau included the Interior Décor Group with velour cloth

For 1978, exterior and interior changes were minor, but there were some major model additions. To begin with, a new Sport Décor Group was unveiled. Originally tagged in trade journals as the Macho package, this option touted simulated rear deck hold-down straps and Polycast wheels. The pinstripes, straps, body side moldings, and Lugano-grained vinyl roof would be offered in a unique Chamois color or black, along with the interior trims of Chamois, Russet, or Saddle. A limited number of colors were offered with the package, including Russet Metallic, Black, Dark Brown metallic, Ember Metallic, Light Chamois, Chamois Glow, and Dark Midnight Blue.

Next among the new models was the closest thing to an open T-Bird since 1966. The T-Roof Convertible used a pair of tinted glass roof panels with an aluminum framework, installed by subcontractor Cars and Concepts. The $750 T-roof was part of a market trend toward removable hatches.

Lastly, the most memorable hatchling in the Thunderbird nest for 1978 was also the most expensive Thunderbird to date. Starting at a whopping $10,106, the Diamond Jubilee Edition was part of Ford's 75th Anniversary celebration, as was a similarly named Lincoln Mark V. Jubilees were offered in Diamond Blue Metallic with a matching, color Valino vinyl roof and velour cloth interior; Ember Metallic with an Ember vinyl roof and Chamois velour interior; and Polar White with either Diamond Blue or Ember vinyl roof and related interior trim. Among the added touches for the Diamond Jubilees were leather-covered dashes, grilles, and trim in color-coordinated accents, and blanked-off quarter windows. The B-pillar window was marked "Diamond Jubilee Edition." Cast-aluminum turbine wheels, pinstriping with dealer-optional monogrammed letters displaying the buyer's initials, a gold-plated limited edition number plaque for the dash, and other little touches distinguished this as a special car. Over 18,000 buyers chose the Diamond Jubilee T-Bird.

The option list for 1978 grew by a handful of items; six new colors were added, and the interior could now be had with a rainbow-inspired cloth and vinyl bucket seat option. To capitalize on the latest fad, designers included a 40-channel Citizens Band radio option. The factory-produced CB used a unique handheld microphone with controls in the handset.

Following its penchant for doing major facelifts at the end of the generation, Ford distinguished the 1979 version from its predecessors. Styled in part by one of the T-Bird's fathers, William "Bill" Boyer, the rear end separated the taillights with a center-mounted back-up light incorporating the word "Thunderbird." The egg-crate grille was modified with larger openings. Nine new exterior colors and two new interior trim colors were added, and a flight-bench seat with fold-down center armrests became standard.

Since Ford wasn't playing up its 76th Anniversary, it replaced the Diamond Jubilee Edition with a Heritage model in new colors. While Ford painted most Heritages Maroon or Light Medium Blue with matching velour trim and vinyl roofs, at mid-year buyers could also choose a Red Glow and Pastel Chamois with maroon trim, Midnight Blue with the blue trim, or Polar White with either of the trims and either white or color-coordinated vinyl tops. All were available in optional two-tone combinations for the lower body and variations of the vinyl roof color. The Sport Décor Group was again offered, as was the T-Roof option.

The eighth generation Thunderbird was one of Ford's bestsellers for the 1970s, helping to keep the company afloat in troubled times. It was also the last frame-on-body T-Bird, the last to offer only a V-8 engine (until the 2002 Thunderbird), and, in Diamond Jubilee trim, the first Ford Division production automobile to retail for over $10,000. The next generation of Thunderbird would continue the movement toward downsizing, but with mixed results.

CHAPTER NINE

1980-1982
Retrenchment—Wrong Place, Wrong Time

T-Bird's 25th anniversary in 1980 was memorialized in the Silver Anniversary Edition, which featured Anniversary Silver Glow metallic paint and black highlights.

(opposite) Metric-sized tires and aluminum TRX wheels were part of the Silver Anniversary Edition and offered through 1982.

The 1980 Silver Anniversary Edition was widely advertised, as seen here.
Alan H. Tast collection

Designed to comply with strict requirements for fuel economy and emissions, the first Thunderbirds of the 1980s became a reminder of how the U.S. automotive industry had failed to keep pace with overseas competitors in offering Americans cars of quality and value.

Ford designers sat down at their drafting tables in 1977 to hash out the Thunderbird that would kick off the 1980s. Several things influenced their design choices. First, Washington was pressing for smaller, stingier cars. Second, engines over five liters for intermediate passenger cars like the T-Bird were on the way out. Third, the company was finalizing a new unibody platform for the Fairmont/Zephyr that could be lengthened and bulked up for the T-Bird/Cougar line.

To begin, product planners reduced the T-Bird's length by 16.8 inches and its wheelbase by 5.6 inches, from 114 to 108.4 inches. With more aluminum and less sheet metal, they dropped 700 pounds of the car's weight, bringing it to 3,300 pounds. For the first time in the car's history, the T-Bird offered an optional inline six-cylinder engine, which displaced 200 cubic inches.

Nobody on the project team could predict that three of the major decision-makers for the new Thunderbird would be gone by the time it hit the dealerships. Company president Lee Iacocca, who pushed for the boxy Thunderbird, was ousted on October 15, 1978, by Chairman Henry Ford II, and replaced by Phillip Caldwell. Henry II turned over the chairmanship to Caldwell on March 13, 1980. Finally, the person ultimately responsible for Ford's design division, Vice President Gene Bordinat, retired in the same period. Iacocca, Henry II, and Bordinat all had a say in the final decision to release the 1980 version for production. In other words, the 1980 T-Bird was the product of men whose vision the company was leaving behind.

Designers under Bill Boyer retained the basket handle roofline with the small B-pillar window on the upper-end cars, while putting a larger pane on the base model. They also carried over the hidden headlights, this time with trim that wrapped around the corner, onto the front fenders, and blended in with the side marker and cornering lights. The body was squared off, while exterior mirrors were fared into the doors. Designers reached consensus on the next generation's look by the spring of 1978, and then turned the design over to engineers to refine the car's aerodynamics. Engineering ran mock-ups through more than 50 hours of wind tunnel testing to make sure the aerodynamics were an improvement over the previous car.

Meanwhile, interior designers scouted for new products to use inside the car. Digital instruments provided a modern touch to the dashboard, while cloth bonded to hardboard

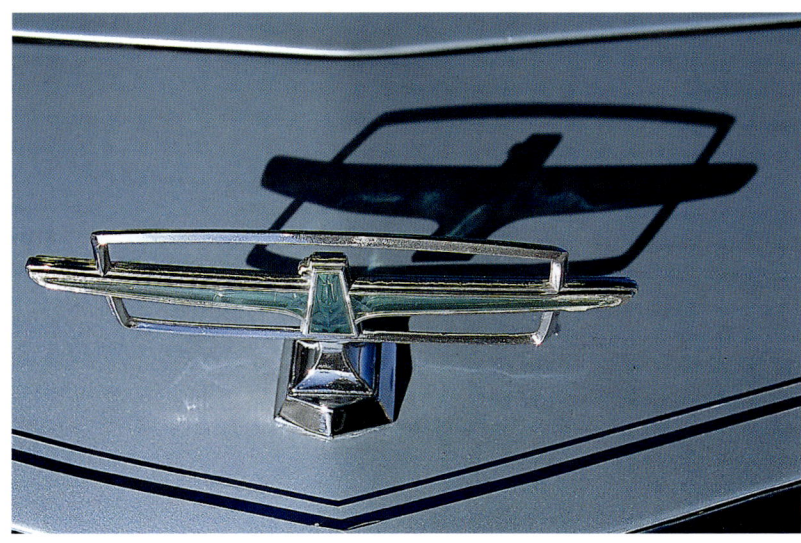

Color-keyed plastic inserts were used on upper-level T-Birds from 1977 through 1982.

The base model T-Birds had a larger B-pillar window, like this 1982 in Vaquero Glow and White.

foam made for a headliner that was lightweight and wouldn't sag (at least not until after the car was a few years old). Still, the new interior was much like the ones before it—a mix of faux woodgrain paneling, vinyl-covered and colored plastic panels, and molded nylon pile carpeting. There were 9 color combinations, including 5 solid colors and 4 with white seats, combined with 10 choices of bench and bucket seats, including Recaro adjustable units in either cloth and vinyl or leather. A total of 62 possible combinations, not including 2 unique selections used with the Silver Anniversary Edition, were available.

Options wizards also developed an externally mounted, five-button "Keyless Entry System," with which owners could gain access to the car by punching in an assigned code. Ford used this system on other higher-end Fords, Mercurys, Lincolns, and on future T-Birds for years to come.

In all, 15 exterior colors were offered, including 10 metallics. Designers did have one thing to key on for 1980: the Thunderbird's 25th Anniversary. Ford made a Silver Anniversary Edition T-Bird, in the appropriate color with Black accents, its top-of-the-line car. Stylists also chose Black with silver accents or Silver Metallic, Red Glow, and Midnight Blue Metallic with silver accents.

The Silver Anniversary T-Bird was a separate model in the line-up and retailed at $11,679 before buyers added anything from a host of options. Fitted with special cast aluminum wheels and Dove Gray cloth or leather interior, the car also had a front-end styling slightly different from the base and Town Landau models with the deletion of the grille below the front bumper. A color-coordinated wrap-over aluminum tiara with Silver Anniversary-scripted B-pillar windows further distinguished the package.

The 302-ci V-8 was the top engine choice. By reducing the bore and stroke of the same engine, Ford offered a lower powered 4.2-liter, 255-ci variant, with 115 horsepower. Ford conceived the 4.2 as a thrifty V-8 alternative to the 302. It became the standard engine in the Town Landau, while the Silver Anniversary cars only had 302s. Though still available, the 351 V-8 did not go to the Thunderbird. Instead, the LTD got the largest Ford engine. Late in the production run, the 200-ci, six-cylinder engine was added.

To supplement its more fuel-efficient engines, Ford produced a transmission with higher gear ratios. The resulting automatic overdrive transmission became a staple of the Ford power team line-up throughout the 1980s. Ford's engineers boasted that adding a fourth gear would increase the car's maximum range on a 20-gallon tank of gas by 100 miles.

A four-spoke steering wheel, with fingertip cruise control and tilt column, frames a simple dash layout for 1982.

Underneath, engineers beefed up the Fairmont's MacPherson strut suspension to handle the heavier Thunderbird.

The automotive press was allowed to see the new Thunderbird for the first time in the summer of 1979. They weren't that impressed. Neither the car's performance nor its quality stood out. Despite lukewarm reviews, the T-Bird still was one of the better sellers for the year, but it was only destined to get worse as confidence in the economy tanked, interest rates reached 20 percent, and people were more willing to put their money in CDs—Certificates of Deposit—which people kept track of on billboards with electronic number displays.

At the beginning of 1980 production, the Chicago Assembly Plant was working overtime to build stocks for dealers. The Lorain, Ohio, plant, which had built exclusively Cougars, was converted to make Thunderbirds, too. But by the time of winter 1979, unsold 1980 models were filling up dealers' lots. Plants even shut down temporarily for "inventory adjustment," as they called it. For what started out as such a promising concept, the T-Bird was in the wrong place at the wrong time.

What was good about the 1980 Thunderbird? For starters, it sold well in comparison to similar intermediates. It was Ford's second best-seller, not counting pickups, behind the downsized-for-1979 LTD. It was a smaller, easier to handle car with power rack and pinion steering. It also had the advantage of being a relative miser on gas with the 200-ci inline 6-cylinder—but only 6,115 were sold with that engine.

For 1981, the Thunderbird received some slight restyling. The chin of plastic eggcrate grillework below the front bumper was gone. Otherwise, it pretty much carried over 1980's specs. There were 14 colors offered, including 10 metallics, and 4 were extra-cost Glamour/Glow colors. The Thunderbird was not available in green. A record-setting 12 seating options in conjunction with 10 upholstery choices (4 of which included white seats) resulted in a total of 83 possible selections.

The mid-range Town Landau returned for 1981. You could also opt for a faux convertible top, called a Carriage Roof, with the base model. No records were kept as to how many were built this way, but you're lucky to see one today. The high-end model was once again the Heritage edition. Engine choices remained the same, but you could get the baby V-8 or the inline-six for the same price. Bad press about the baby V-8 prompted 16 percent of buyers to take the inline six-cylinder engine. Production declined by almost half from 1980's respectable level of 156,803 units to 86,693.

A token performance option was the Michelin TRX steel-belted P-metric radials, which were also offered in 1980. These required a special TR aluminum wheel. While this was touted as a performance upgrade, buyers regarded it as the kiss of death. The tires were much more expensive than conventional radials, and the wheels were a very expensive unit. Not many people chose this wheel-tire combination.

The biggest news for the 1982 model was the deletion of the 302 and the addition of the 3.8 Liter/232-ci V-6—an all-new mill that would become a Ford mainstay almost to the end of the twentieth century. The V-6 was offered only in the base and Town Landau models, and co-existed with the inline-six until late in the calendar year, when the latter disappeared. The two sixes accounted for just under 40 percent of 1982 sales, with the 255 V-8 accounting for the remaining 27,717 cars. With only 45,412 examples, 1982 was one of the worst years for T-Bird sales.

Nobody at Ford in June 1978, during the height of their Diamond Jubilee celebrations, could have imagined things going so far awry so quickly. The bad thing about automotive product cycles is that once you're committed to a three- or four-year plan and invest hundreds of millions of dollars to develop tooling, arrange for subcontractors to supply parts, develop and refine engineering, and attempt to predict what fabric choices will be popular three years out, there's no turning back. From 1980 to 1981, sales dropped by about half. They did it again for 1982. It was time for the Bird to molt.

The last year for the econobox was 1982, which brought an end to another chapter in the life of the T-Bird.

CHAPTER TEN

1983–1986
Aero Coup

The 1983–1986 Turbo Coupes came standard with a manual five-speed transmission. An automatic transmission was not available until 1984.

(opposite) A light-colored grid serves as a background for the instruments on the early Turbo Coupes.

The mid-1980s Monte Carlos in SS garb battled their way into the aero wars with a sloped front nose. A limited number of SS models, as well as Pontiac Grand Prix's, received a sloped rear window to create a fastback-like version to compete with T-Birds in NASCAR. Alan H. Tast collection

Revolutionary ideas are those that run counter to accepted thought. Challenge the status quo. Shake things up. The tenth manifestation of the Thunderbird did all the above, and more.

Times were tough at Ford: there were no large budgets or cash reserves available to start a project from the ground up. Designers had to be resourceful to turn the Thunderbird around. They had to use bits and pieces from established lines. Fortunately, there was plenty around to work with. For the body substructure, they could combine the Fox (Mustang) platform's front stampings and the rear from the Lincoln Continental—the resulting wheelbase was virtually the same as the original 1955 Thunderbird. (Of course, by the early 1980s there was more car hanging out beyond the front and rear wheels.)

Design work on the Aerobird began in the winter of 1978–1979—a rather long lead time for a model not scheduled for release until early 1983. Designers and engineers needed a longer timeframe to reduce the car's drag coefficient to a target figure of 0.35. The new Lincoln Continental Mark VII coupe design, with its rounded and sloped lines, offered the T-Bird's designers a fresh perspective.

Designers also benefited from advances in computer technology that made their calculations easier and quicker, and allowed them to save development costs by modeling ideas onscreen.

The Thunderbird that emerged had simpler, softer-edged design than its predecessor. Aircraft-style doors wrapped over the sides of the roof allowed engineers to do away with the drip rail, a feature that had been nearly ubiquitous across manufacturers since the beginning of the twentieth century. The seam between the roof and quarter panels was moved to align with the top of the doors and filled to remove the channel between panels. In the rear, a ducktail-like kick-up of the feature line produced a very subtle spoiler on the rear decklid. Canting the back face forward also allowed the airstream to pass over the rear end without creating a turbulent low-pressure area.

Between the doors, about the only thing retained from the prior "econobox" was the optional electronic instrument panel, made standard on the Heritage model. Bucket seats and a center floor-mounted console returned to the standard equipment list, with no bench seat available. Trims came in the typical range of vinyl for the less-expensive version, with upgrades to super-soft vinyl, velour, or leather. Twelve color combinations were offered over the six choices for seats/upholstery, including several that were unique for the super-soft vinyl trim.

The dash panel stretched across the width of the car with a narrow opening for the instruments, while the lower center extension contained the climate controls and audio system. The console had a built-in ashtray, housed control switches for power windows when installed, and in a raised rear section provided a storage bin with a padded lid that doubled as a center armrest. Steering wheels carried over 1982's four-spoke design, with a unique center pad on the Turbo Coupe. The new shell, when fitted with 14-inch wheels and radial tires, stood at 53.2 inches high, stretched out over 197.6 inches from tip to tail, and was 0.9-inches shy of 6 feet in width

The Turbo Coupe provided increased power without larger displacement or more cylinders. Yet there were downsides to turbocharging. First was a momentary lag

This is an advertisement for the 1984 FILA Edition. Alan H. Tast collection

(above) The 1983–1986 models were developed to cheat the wind better than any previous T-Bird and were touted to have a coefficient of drag of only 0.36, making them a favorite of racers from stock cars to the drags.

(right) FILA emblems were used on the front fenders, and its painted aluminum wheels were another unique feature.

(opposite) The 1985 and 1986 T-birds, such as this 1985 FILA Edition, had revised taillights to move the back-up lights inboard.

before the turbo spooled up to deliver its power boost. The turbo also required adequate oiling to avoid seizure. Finally, turbos produced heat that could undercut their own gains, as hot air holds less oxygen and therefore burns less efficiently than cooler air.

The turbocharged engine was based on Ford's 140-ci/2.3-liter four-cylinder overhead camshaft engine used in applications such as the Mustang. What it did for the bottom line was amazing when compared to the T-Bird's normally aspirated engines—the 3.8-liter V-6 and 302-ci/5.0-liter pushrod V-8. The turbo produced 142 horsepower at 5,000 rpm with a net torque of 172 foot-pounds at 3,800 rpm. The V-6, even though it was 1,500 cc larger, made only 110 horsepower at 3,800 rpm, and just three more foot-pounds of torque than the turbo, at 2,000 rpm. The turbo even topped the electronically fuel-injected 302's 130 horsepower. The small-block V-8 surpassed it handily in torque, however, with 240 foot-pounds at 2,000 rpm. Ford's fourth-generation Electronic Engine Control (EEC-IV) onboard computer regulated timing to keep the T-Bird running smoothly.

Buyers could choose either the standard SelectShift three-speed automatic with a locking torque converter, or the automatic overdrive transmission that had been around since 1980, for models other than the Turbo Coupe. The sporty Turbo featured the Borg Warner T-5 five-speed manual gearbox exclusively. Variable-ratio rack-and-pinion steering was standard on all models except the Turbo Coupe or cars with the TRX package.

Outside the Turbo Coupe wore simple "EFI Turbo" badges on the front fenders, blacked-out headlight bezels, and two driving lights in the lower bumper fascia. Inside, only the TC got blacked-out dash trim, surrounding a full analog gauge package with tachometer, oil pressure, and coolant temperature. A separate boost gauge appeared where the clock was fitted on the base and Heritage models. Standard seats in the Turbo were adjustable for seat-back angle, plus lumbar and thigh support. Underneath, four nitrogen-charged shock absorbers—two for up-and-down damping and two for fore-and-aft movement—comprised the QuadraShock rear suspension system. Goodyear Eagle P205/70HR14 blackwall tires on 8-hole cast aluminum rims connected the car to the road. The base price for the Turbo Coupe was $11,790.

The base Thunderbird, which retailed for $9,197 without options, was fitted with a two-barrel, 3.8-liter V-6. The EFI 302 V-8 cost $288 more. Standard exterior side trim featured wide, vinyl rub strips topped with a bright silver mylar insert on the bumpers and quarters. Base wheel covers were made of a rubberized composition. If the Exterior Accent Group was installed, the narrow strip between the wheel arches was given the wide moldings, and Luxury stainless-steel wheel covers replaced the plastic ones.

A long list of options was available. For the performance enthusiast, aside from the 5.0-liter V-8, there again was Traction-Lok for the rear axle, and a choice of wheels and tires. The TRX package of P-metric Michelin radial tires and tri-pattern aluminum wheels could replace the standard P195/75R14 all-season white sidewall tires and deluxe wheel covers. The Turbo Coupe's standard P205/70HR14 blackwall performance tires were available on the base and Heritage cars. Wheel cover choices included a stainless-steel cover with a plastic T-Bird center emblem, a simulated wire wheel cover, and a multi-spoked styled road wheel. An old-style pivoting vent window was optional, but few buyers went for it.

The Heritage commanded a whopping $3,031 premium over the standard coupe. Part of the reason for this was all the features that came with the Heritage package. They included the Interior Luxury Group, with velour-covered seats, and map pockets in the doors and behind the front seat backs. A carpeted trunk, woodtone appliqués on the dash and steering wheel center, lighted mirrors in the sun visors, 16-ounce cut-pile carpeting, air conditioning, power windows, and remote-control exterior rearview mirrors added to the package. Above the heater control head was an array of warning lights for an open door, brake and headlight status, and low fuel and windshield washer fluid levels. In the center of the panel, which spanned the width of the dash, was a digital clock or optional Tripminder computer.

Heritage models featured a special emblem on the C-pillar, an illuminated rectangular electroluminescent coach lamp. Regretfully, these often burned out early in the car's life and since there was no easy way to replace them, they usually stayed dark. Early brochures also showed the word "Heritage" silk-screened onto the B-pillar window.

The standard coupe and the Turbo Coupe used a newly styled Bird emblem with a linear outline, which was repeated at the top of the grille and on the rear taillight lenses.

The general public had no idea what was coming when the new Thunderbird was finally released on February 17, 1983. The Turbo Coupe did not bow until April Fool's Day, as last-minute problems were ironed out. To say that the public was excited about it is an understatement: By the time the model year ended, almost 110,000 base model and Heritage coupes were built, with another 12,566 Turbo Coupes swelling the total to 121,999 units—nearly three times as many as the 1982!

For 1984, Ford restructured the fancy model and added another high-end glamour package. The Heritage became the Élan, a name intended to evoke European sophistication and perhaps comparisons to BMW, which was rapidly becoming popular with well-heeled yuppies. A new, more contemporary steering wheel was introduced with two downward-sloped spokes to allow full visibility of the instrument cluster and either analog or optional electronic

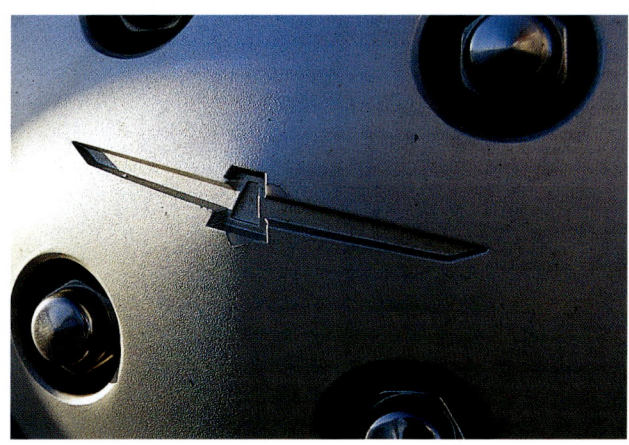

(opposite) A lineup of Aerobirds, including a 1983 Turbo Coupe, 1985 FILA, and base model.

(below) Styled road wheels for 1983–1986 featured a T-Bird emblem in the center. They were not available on Turbo Coupes and FILAs.

Aerobirds were bred for speed and they look right at home on the race track

gauges. When speed (cruise) control was installed, fingertip controls were located in the spokes. The Turbo Coupe kept the four-spoke, leather-wrapped rim from the previous year.

Also adding cache to the line-up was the FILA edition, another European connection—this time to an Italian sports apparel manufacturer. Stylists incorporated the FILA theme with special badging and a unique color combination using charcoal gray body accents, along with a light gray body and matching powder-coated aluminum wheels. Red and blue pinstripes to match the FILA logo colors were pulled across the hood and body feature line. The interior also received special appointments with white leather or charcoal gray suede-like seating surfaces.

Powertrain improvements for the V-6 included the switch from carburetion to throttle-body fuel injection, with a horsepower jump to 120 at 3,600 rpm. The 5.0-liter and Turbo Four also offered fuel injection, with the V-8 using a system similar to the V-6. Non-shifting drivers could now order the Turbo Coupe with optional SelectShift automatic. The FILA had the automatic overdrive as standard equipment, while the base and Élan models included it at extra cost for both the 3.8- and 5.0-liter engines.

For the first time, the base model Thunderbird broke the $10,000 ceiling without options, while the FILA topped the $15,000 mark at the upper end. Turbo Coupes could be purchased for $13,820 with the five-speed transmission. Even with the price increases, people were gobbling up the car more so than the year before. A total of

155,866 base coupes, FILAs, and Elans combined were built, of which about a third had the 5.0-liter V-8. With another 14,667 Turbo Coupes joining the tally, this would be another very good year for dealers. It was the bestselling Thunderbird of the 1980s, and the fourth bestselling of all time, following 1977–1979 Birds.

Ford had settled into a long production run for this generation, in part to minimize expenditures and plow the savings into a new Ford that would become as important to the Company as the Models T and A: the Taurus.

There were some significant changes for the 1985 versions, primarily cosmetic. Artists developed a new logo with feathered wings and a wide wingspan. This emblem would become the most-used of all the Thunderbird trademarks, gracing all T-Birds through the 1997 model. The change in emblems also affected the taillights. The backup lights were moved inboard to avoid the solid emblems, and a chrome strip was added to the bottom of the lenses.

For the Turbo Coupe, stylists achieved a stealthier monochromatic look by painting the grille the same as the body color. Window moldings were now blacked out. The body side moldings had "Turbo Coupe" embossed at the forward end of the doors, doing away with the small, nondescript badges on the front fenders used the previous two years. These moldings also received a colored inset stripe in lieu of the mylar insert on normally aspirated cars. The TC also got a new steering wheel with a round center hub and two splayed spokes spread out wider than the one used in the other 'Birds.

The dashboard for all models was updated by truncating the instrument panel recess over the top of the center stack. A new, optional digital instrument cluster was also introduced. Cars with split-bench seats used a shorter, flatter consolette in place of the full-length console. A leather-wrapped version of the standard steering wheel was also available.

Standard P205/70R14 tires replaced the previous P195s, while the Turbo Coupe got larger and wider P225/60VR15 tires and aluminum wheels with 10 semicircular holes. The TRX

The 1984 Turbo Coupe promoted the addition of automatic transmission. Alan H. Tast collection

package was gone, but the styled road wheels and locking wire wheel covers were still around, while the luxury wheel covers lost their plastic insert in favor of a raised emblem. White sidewall tires were not offered, bringing to an end a tradition going back to the beginning of the nameplate.

Once again, four models were available, including the Elan and FILA editions. The FILA offered a wider selection of colors, including black, red, or a repeat of the two-tone Pastel Charcoal over Dark Charcoal. Like the year before, it came standard with the automatic overdrive and either suede- or leather-shod bucket seats with full console.

Mechanical revisions for 1985 were limited. The 5.0-liter was now backed up exclusively by the automatic overdrive transmission. When the Turbo Coupe was given the five-speed, its rated output increased by 10 ponies. Electronic boost control was added for the turbocharger. The variable-ratio steering was replaced with a fixed 20:1 ratio gearbox.

Collectors had something to look forward to by January 1985, when Ford released a 30th Anniversary Edition coupe. The 30th Anniversary version blended Turbo Coupe styling and suspension with the EFI 5.0-liter V-8 and AOD transmission, in a Regatta Blue color scheme. Special 30th Anniversary emblems were provided on the rear deck lid, along with special keys showing both a 1955 and 1985 in profile. Buyers also received a goodie bag's worth of promotional items, including a Regatta Blue-colored Members' Only jacket, tote bag, keychain, a booklet on the 30-year history of the marque, and some other premium items. A total of 5,000 were manufactured.

Even with the refinements for 1985, sales slid backward for all models except the Turbo Coupe, to 151,851 units—almost 20,000 less than 1984. The Turbo Coupe had 20,084 examples burning up the streets, an increase of almost a third. Buyers opted for the V-8 engine in over a third of production, or 52,085 cars.

Now entering a fourth year of production in the same shell, the 1986 Thunderbird offered very few earth-shattering changes. The FILA was dropped from the line-up, leaving just the base model, Elan, and Turbo Coupe to do battle against Chevy's Monte Carlo—which was also growing long in the tooth with the same basic 1978-ish body. The major spotting feature for 1986 Bird-watchers was a grille focused more on horizontal elements, and a third brake light on the package tray in the rear window. There were few noteworthy option changes. The flip-up sunroof was dropped in favor of a power-retracted moonroof. A space-saver spare replaced the full-size version.

Running gear did get more power. The central fuel injection system, which looked similar to a carburetor at first glance, was gone. In its place was the Sequential Multipoint Electronic System, which along with an increase in compression to 8.9:1, helped to raise output for the 5.0-liter to 150 horsepower at 3,400 rpm and 270 foot-pounds of torque at 2,000 rpm. Even the four-banger got a boost in output to hit a peak of 155 horse-

Bill Boyer, one of the men most identified with the Thunderbird's design from the 1950s through the early 1980s, poses with a 1985 30th Anniversary Edition. Courtesy Bruce Caswell

power at 4,600 rpm, and another 10 for good measure with the five-speed and clutch.

This time sales rose over 1985, by over 12,000 copies, for a total of 142,650 base-model and Elan coupes. Turbo Coupes also posted a modest gain of less than 1,000 to end the generation's run at 21,315 examples, for total sales of almost 164,000. This would be the second-bestselling year for the T-Bird of the 1980s, and the fifth-bestselling one of all time

The mid-1980s was a good time to be into new cars. Muscle was working its way back into Detroit's products. Cars were now looking exciting and acting the same. And, with the economy turning around, it was less of a strain to buy a new Thunderbird. The next rendition of the winged wonder would have the automotive world stand up and take notice.

CHAPTER ELEVEN

1987–1988
Raw, but Refined

The 1987–1988 Sport lacked special ornamentation.

(opposite) The 1987–1988 Sport came standard with a floor-shifted automatic overdrive transmission.

The success of the Euro-influenced 1983–1986 Thunderbird was a very welcome turn of events for Ford. Buyers' positive reaction to the Aerobird's styling meant that there was little need to tinker with a proven performer.

So, how do you make improvements on a proven winner? Ford's product planners and engineers wrestled with this conundrum in the mid-1980s. The basic body shell that so much R&D effort was expended on was still sound and had some more years left in it, but the exterior skin was probably not going to last much longer without some major revisions. The fear of bringing out a dated design wasn't as much on peoples' minds as providing a fresh image for the marque. After all, consumer attention span was getting shorter in the age of MTV, personal computers, and video games.

Upper management wanted to proceed with only moderate changes to the outer shell and limited updating the passenger compartment. Designers penned changes that stretched the wheelbase just over 3/8ths of an inch to 104.2 inches, and the overall length of the car 5.5 inches to make it 202.1 inches from tail to the extended forward prow. Height, body, and tread width were unchanged from previous years.

There would be a pronounced difference in styling between the Turbo Coupe and other models. Taking a more aggressive stance, the TC could be instantly recognized by its solid urethane nose, which with the large feathered Bird emblem, accentuated the prow. Driving lights, a Turbo Coupe standard, were mounted in the lower valance with the license plate opening and three narrow slots for air supply to the radiator. A pair of functional intake slots was carved out of the hood for the turbocharger intercooler. Side trim had unique color-coordinated inserts and "Turbo Coupe" molded into them, and the rear deck lid received badging on the left side. Door handles, lock bezels, and window trim were blacked out.

In contrast, the other models had a more traditional, bright-plated plastic grille between the aerodynamic head/marker light assemblies, and bright metal trim for the windows and body hardware. The rear taillights, shared by all models, had the twin Thunderbird emblem theme repeated, but the panel assembly had for many die-hard Blue Oval purists something of a Chevrolet-like quality. Even though it was housed in a blackout-style lens, three round openings on each side for the turn signals and brake lights recalled the Impala/Caprice-style tri-lens pattern.

Ford's Motorsports and Special Vehicle Operations (SVO) programs provided ways for buyers seeking something stronger than showroom stock to beef up their own rides. Once again, Ford was offering factory-engineered and race-tested parts to customers with off-street interests, such as drag racing. Engineers were also looking at ways to increase performance in the stock Thunderbirds. The turbo four especially had their attention.

Forcing air into the engine with an exhaust-driven turbine was a proven means of increasing power. Yet, hot air—the only type coming from the exhaust system—was less dense and therefore less effective for combustion than cool air. Ford engineers had solved this problem on the turbo Mustang, back in 1983, with an intercooler that chilled the air before it reentered the engine. Unfortunately, the original 1983–1986 Thunderbird Turbo Coupe was engineered before this was ready, and its engine bay didn't have room for the heat exchanger. For the 1987 version, engineers made the necessary modifications. The intercooler added a whopping 35 horses to the five-speed Turbo Coupe and increased the torque rating to 240 foot-pounds at 3,400 revs. With automatic overdrive, output dropped to 150 ponies and 200 foot-pounds at 3,000 turns per minute.

To provide "whoa" for all that power, engineers fitted disc brakes all around. To prevent lock-up, they put sensors at each corner wired to an onboard computer with the power to regulate hydraulic pressure at each brake. This system, known as antilock brakes (ABS), would become standard on many cars years later—but the Turbo Coupe had it first.

Another advance over the past was Automatic Ride Control, whose censors detected how

The Thunderbird Sport was featured in this ad in 1987. Alan H. Tast collection

Selection as 1987s "Car of the Year" by Motor Trend *delivered well-earned bragging rights to the Turbo Coupe.* Alan H. Tast collection

fast the car was being driven, and resulting cornering and braking forces. It would then send signals to the shock absorbers and struts through a set of solenoids and valves similar to the ABS system, regulating how much pressure should be applied to the dampers. As driving technique became more aggressive, the computer directed the shocks to get stiffer. A switch on the console allowed the driver to set the suspension for a "smooth" or "hard" ride. Automatic Ride Control and antilock brakes were exclusive to the Turbo Coupe, but the Quadra-Link suspension for the rear axle was not. The four-shock setup was made standard for a new model, simply called Thunderbird Sport.

The Sport was not as well-equipped as a Turbo Coupe or the replacement for the Elan, called the LX. What the Sport offered over the base model was traditional muscle car value. Only available with the 150-horse 5.0-liter and automatic overdrive, the Sport had some unique features. It came standard with speed-rated P215HR70 tires supported by 14-inch styled road wheels. Not only did it have the Quadra-Link rear suspension, but it also had heavy-duty sway bars and springs. Badging was not provided for it, other than the black body side trim with silver mylar inserts and an emblem on the rear. A revised electronic instrument panel was also mandatory for the Sport, and optional on the standard coupe and LX. Unique to the Sport was a floor-mounted shifter for the automatic overdrive. The V-8 increased the unsprung weight of the car, which tipped the scales at 3,315 pounds, making it the heaviest of the 1987 T-Birds: The Turbo Coupe was 3,419 pounds with the AOD, while the base model was the lightweight with a V-6 at 3,133 pounds.

At the top of the luxury heap was the LX. A new designation for the high-trim Thunderbird, the LX came standard with a lot of things that were options on the Sport and base model. While the standard model had a reclining cloth or split-bench seat with the consolette, the LX used a velour-like luxury cloth with a different insert pattern. Like the Turbo Coupe, it had a leather-wrapped steering wheel with a circular center horn pad and two horizontal spokes below the wheel's center line, along with a tilting function. A heavier-weight 24-ounce cut pile carpet made under-foot areas plusher not only for the LX, but also for the Turbo Coupe. For convenience, interval wipers, power windows and door locks, digital clock, and automatic parking brake release were added. Courtesy lights throughout the car and in the trunk, as well as under the bonnet, were supplemented by the illuminated entry system, which lit up the door locks when the chrome-plated exterior door handle was lifted. For occupants' listening variety, the standard AM/FM stereo radio included a cassette tape player. Wood-tone inserts were also unique to the LX; the Turbo Coupe used a brushed aluminum appliqué. For the four corners meeting the pavement, the LX used styled road wheels and P215/70Rx14 blackwall tires. Heated driver and passenger seats were available only with the LX. The Systems Sentry/Diagnostic Warning Light package was also standard on the LX, as well as the Turbo Coupe.

Wheels and tires were all new for the Turbo Coupe. Nicknamed "snowflake" wheels, their 16-inch diameter rims wore Goodyear Gatorback P225/60VR unidirectional speed-rated tires. The others used 14-inch diameter rims, including the aluminum 8-hole cast aluminum

wheel and styled road wheel, or the steel wheel with optional locking wire wheel cover.

Under a new concept called the Preferred Equipment Package, Ford grouped popular options for each model, helping to keep production costs down and make the cars' pricing more competitive with such rivals as the Monte Carlo and Pontiac Bonneville.

The new Turbo Coupe generated a strong buzz when Ford introduced its full line on October 2, 1986. Performance buffs were wowed by the TC's increased capabilities. *Motor Trend* even crowned it Car of the Year. MT's drivers placed the Turbo Coupe head-to-head with a Chrysler LeBaron and Pontiac Bonneville, along with compacts Dodge Shadow and Plymouth Sundance, then slalomed, drag-raced, and panic-stopped all of them to evaluate

The Turbo Coupe received unique snowflake wheels, as shown on this 1988 Medium Red Clearcoat Metallic Turbo Coupe.

their performance. In the standing quarter mile, the TC ran 16.48 seconds at a speed of 85.1 miles per hour. This was not in the same class as a 1960s muscle car, but the critics were impressed elsewhere—for example, with the braking system's ability to pull down the car from 60 miles an hour to 0 in 130 feet, and with the automatic ride control. All the high-tech goodies led one writer to call the Turbo Coupe "an electronic dream machine."

Even with the improvements and recognition, the number of takers for the 1987s declined from the previous year. A total of 128,135 T-Birds of all models were shipped out of the Lorain Assembly Plant, including 23,812 Turbo Coupes.

The end of the Turbo era would come with the 1988 model year, concluding a six-year run. There were no major changes in store, other than semi-dual exhaust for the Sport to

add 5 horsepower and let it breathe easier. The Sport also shared instrumentation with the Turbo Coupe, relegating the electronic instruments option to the base and LX as part of the Electronic Equipment Group. Even though prices went up to $13,166 for a base model with a V-6 at the low end and $16,606 for the LX with a V-8, not including options, sales did increase by almost 20,000 cars for a total of 147,243 examples of all models. The Turbo Coupe had its best year ever, exiting the stage at the hands of 36,811 buyers. Unknown to Ford at the time, sales would never reach these levels again, though they would come close in the mid-1990s.

In all the years of Thunderbird production, there were only two generations with such a short run, 1970–1971 and 1987–1988. Both shared body structures and interiors with a previous generation, but the 1987–1988s managed to become standouts because of the advances the Turbo Coupe blazed for the rest of the line-up. Thunderbird was holding on as the technological innovator for the Ford product catalog, and the next round of development would yield one of the longest lived platforms in company history.

(left) To identify the 1987–1988 Turbo Coupe from the rear, a nameplate was placed above the left side taillight.

(below) A small radiator mounted beside the engine gives this car away as an intercooled 1987–1988 Turbo Coupe.

CHAPTER TWELVE

1989–1997

Super

The T-Bird's 35th anniversary was marked by offering a Super Coupe in a unique black-blue-light titanium color scheme.

(right) The Super Coupe received its name thanks to the supercharger sitting on top of the 3.8-liter V-6.

(opposite) Special emblems were used on the front fenders to identify 35th anniversary editions.

Thunderbird was enjoying a very comfortable position going into its 34th continuous year of production. The raving of the enthusiast press for the Turbo Coupe and its emphasis on performance brought street cred back to something other than the Mustang, now going on its 10th year on the Fox-body platform. Thunderbird had spent the last six years refining its S-body platform, but new developments in powerplant design would require a new structure that could carry forward with minimal rework for at least the same amount of time.

The heart of the new Thunderbird would be the 3.8-liter V-6, exclusively. Now engineers began working on ways to wring more horsepower from it. Turbocharging had paid off in the four-cylinder turbo coupe, but lag and temperature control were persistent concerns. Instead, engineers turned to another venerable means of forced induction, this one with no lag and with power across the rpm band: supercharging. Not the stand-alone-centrifugal type like the McCullough/Paxton-style associated with the 1957 Ford/Thunderbird and

The 1989 Cougar XR-7 continued the squared-off rear window motif and sported the same supercharged V-6 as the T-Bird through 1990. Alan H. Tast collection

Calling attention to the T-Bird's history, ads for the 35th Anniversary Edition boldly stated many enthusiasts' thoughts.
Alan H. Tast collection

favored by Mustang/Shelby owners, though. The centrifugal blower required more room in front of the engine—room being taken up by an alternator, smog pump, water pump, air conditioning compressor, and the serpentine drive belt system. Something a little more direct in application was called for.

The better way to handle air management would be from the top of the block. And the tried-and-true method to do this was with a Roots-type design. The Roots blower system used a pair of intermeshed, horizontally arranged rotors housed inside a cast-aluminum housing, with the drive rotor connected to a pulley spun by a drive belt.

Hot rodders had known about this kind of blower since the early 1950s, when a Romanian-born engineer by the name of Zora Arkus-Duntov adapted the supercharger from a GMC truck engine for a Ford flathead V-8. The Thunderbird's blower had to sit under the hood, and preferably under the same hood that the regular V-6 would use. As good fortune would have it, Eaton Corporation had been promoting a positive-displacement blower to the Company since 1977. The time was now right to try out what Eaton referred to as the M90.

The M90 took a page from the Turbo Coupe and incorporated both fuel injection and an intercooler. Air was pulled into the system through a ribbed plastic tube from the air filter box through a sensor-monitored throttle body. Once past the throttle body, the air stream fed directly into the spinning rotors, where it was compressed between the blades and the blower case. The air, compressed at a 12-to-1 ratio, rushed up and out through a cast-aluminum bonnet and tube into the intercooler, which was mounted next to the radiator, and back to the rear of the intake manifold through another cast aluminum tube. The compressed air then filled each of the six cylinders and mixed with fuel squirted into the bores from individual injectors. Ford engineers continuously refined the system from prototypes through the mid-1990s. The primary refinement, to reduce blower whine, was a tri-blade rotor fabricated with a 60-degree twist for a tightly intermeshed pattern.

There were numerous differences between the supercharged and regular V-6s. The normally aspirated V-6 used a traditional distributor with the EEC-IV system, a cooling fan mounted on the end of the water pump shaft/pulley, and an aluminum cross-flow radiator. The supercharged V-6 used a distributor-less setup with a remote-mounted ignition coil pack and distribution block for the plug wires, timed to fire through the Distributorless Ignition System (DIS) module connected to a camshaft sensor, crankshaft sensor, and the EEC-IV module. It also used a copper and brass downflow radiator, unlike the standard V-6.

The team of stylists and designers, led by Dave Turner, Allen Ornes, Ted Finney, as well as others, probably didn't realize in the summer of 1983, when work began on the MN-12, that it would end up like it did. Early styling concepts focused on front-wheel-drive packages to in essence create a two-door Taurus, or a larger version of what was supposed to replace the Mustang, the Probe. Further into the design stages, futuristic dreams were refined into workable, buildable concepts that could be mocked up for evaluation and testing. The gestation period for the new body went well into 1985 before it finally became solid enough for engineering to really take off. In defiance of current trends, front-wheel drive was discarded and the live rear axle and driveshaft were retained by the time it received approval for production.

The engine bay, since it didn't need to contain an eight-piston block, was shortened to snuggle around the smaller V-6. To stabilize the car, front and rear wheels were moved closer to the ends to provide a 113-inch wheelbase, nearly matching the 1958–1966 cars. A return to drag-strut technology to hold the lower front suspension arms in place, paired with a true independent rear suspension with half-shafts to drive the rear wheels, allowed for a more-positive handling experience when combined with beefier sway bars and variable-rate springs. To point the car in the right direction, variable-ratio power steering was incorporated with the assistance of microprocessors and sensors. This automatically adjusted the "feel" of the steering as speed changed: as one drove faster, more effort was required to turn the wheel, unless there was a sudden turn of the wheel needed for an emergency situation, at which time full power assist returned.

External differences were plenty between the entry-level, LX, and Super Coupe models. Front fascias for the sedate versions had multiple slots on each side to conceal the air intakes, while on the Super Coupe they had two large openings with an embossed "SC" in the center. Side moldings were narrow black strips of vinyl on the SC, wider with silver mylar inserts for the others. At the rear, the taillights had a place on the bottom for the Thunderbird nameplate, with "LX" added for the more luxurious option. When the supercharger was in place, the nameplate was omitted: the bumper cover was embossed with "Thunderbird SC." Lower body ground effect panels were used on the SC and wrapped around the lower body, with openings in the front and rear bumper covers faired to match the body appliqués. A set of driving lights was placed at the outboard edges of the front bumper's lower opening.

The interiors of the MN-12 were 10 percent larger than the S-body cars from 1983–1988. Driver and front-passenger seating for all versions was limited to buckets with a full-length console separating the two front passengers, returning to the late 1950s concept and doing away with the bench seat. The Super Coupe went above and beyond the lesser versions by offering an articulated version with adjustments for thighs, back, and sides, as well as a fold-down rear cushion to allow for hauling long items like skis. Dashes differed just as in the previous version, with the Super Coupe getting a performance cluster with analog instruments including oil pressure and boost gauges along with a tachometer, while the LX could be had with an optional electronic instrument display. The standard car got a simpler cluster with fuel and temperature gauges flanking the speedometer, and warning lights for oil pressure, door ajar, seat belts, check engine, brake system, charging system, and optional anti-theft alarm and anti-lock brakes. A new passive restraint system was developed with shoulder belts that slid automatically on a track following the door opening, moving forward when the door was opened and pulled against the seat occupant when the door was closed. This system would be abandoned by 1993.

Breaking with the tradition of fall launches, marketers decided to provide the public with a late Christmas present on the day after Christmas, 1988. The Super Coupe wowed

Super Coupes from 1989 through 1991 had a unique bumper cover with embossed "SC" logo and dual intake openings. The covers, minus the "SC" were used for all 1992–1993 models.

(above) The 1992 Thunderbird received the bumper cover from the Super Coupe as part of its facelift, along with revised side moldings.

(right) The 5.0-liter V-8 was brought back by popular demand in 1991, but had to be modified to fit the V-6-sized engine bay. The 5.0-liter was used through 1993.

virtually every critic with its power, throttle response, and handling, aided by a new generation of Automatic Ride Control used in the last iteration of the Turbo Coupe. Pundits marveled at how the SC could keep up with the best BMWs and other European road cars with typical American frugality. Buyers must have liked the value too because 122,909 were spoken for. Of that total, there were 12,809 SCs built with a five-speed gearbox and another 8,041 with the automatic. However, disturbingly enough, these numbers were down from 1988 figures. Part of this could be attributed to the late launch, but there were signals that even though it was a new car, the appeal of a rear-wheel-drive coupe was on the decline.

For the 1990 model run, there were few modifications. Enthusiasts were treated to a stunning black, silver, and blue 35th Anniversary Super Coupe with a gray-suede and black-leather bolstered interior. The 35th Anniversary car was visually distinctive with its special blue-and-chrome cloisonné fender badge, titanium silver lower body, wide side trim with blue inserts, and the black clearcoat body, as well as the cast-aluminum five-spoke wheels. As with the 30th Anniversary car before it, buyers received a goodie bag full of 35th Anniversary-related items such as key chains, gym bags, a special interior care kit for the suede inserts, literature, and other trinkets.

Ford intended to build 5,000 Anniversary cars, but accounting at the end of the year could show only that 3,371 examples were produced. These were part of a total run of 114,040, including 28,033 Super Coupes of both automatic and five-speed persuasion—the most prevalent SC ever built. The LX and base model combined totaled 82,636. The decline of almost 9,000 T-Birds from the previous year was probably a bit of a surprise, but not totally unexpected. Planners were so optimistic on the future of the car that they announced long-range plans like a six-speed transmission for 1994, and a new body for 1996. There was confidence this 'Bird had wings and legs to carry it through the 1990s.

The next year of the series had some adjustments, but the major one for 1991 was a return of the V-8. Since the introduction of the SC, more than a few people bombarded dealers to voice their displeasure in the replacement for displacement. In order to get the 5.0-liter back into the 'Bird, engineers had to shrink it with a shortened water pump and timing chain cover. When provided with other features like a lower-tech suspension setup of stiffer springs and bigger stabilizer bars, it became known as the Sport option. Badges on the front fenders promoted the V-8's return.

Production for 1991 included 59,543 base and LX types with the 3.8-liter, 16,232 with the 5.0 HO (including 2,976 Sports), plus an additional 8,944 SCs. The total run of 84,719 was down almost 20,000 from the year before.

One of the T-Bird's innovations was a fully electronic instrument cluster, shown here in a 1992 model.

Body restyling was very subtle for 1992, with curves over the rear taillights instead of the previous straight lines. High-tech arrived for the taillights with light-emitting diodes (LEDS) replacing conventional light bulbs. The Sport with its V-8 received full recognition as a separate model, rather than as an option package. All models got the SC-type front bumper cover and a smoothed out center section. Side moldings were shaped like an arrow from behind the front wheel arch, widening out as they went toward the rear. They were also given a short, bright mylar insert in the portion of the spear behind the door, which continued behind the rear wheel arch around the rear bumper cover. The Super Coupe retained the narrow rub strip, open rear fascia, and conservative ground effect add-ons of the past three years. Underneath, exhaust systems became less restrictive due to changes in the gas tank that allowed some rerouting of pipes.

A major change in the front-end styling of T-Bird happened in 1994 with a center opening in the nose for the radiator and pronounced lower bumper cover.

Net results at the end of the year would again show a drift downward in demand, with 75,149 of all styles rolling out of Lorain and into showrooms around the world. The Sport had a total of 7,074, over three times the number ordered in 1991, but the Super Coupe couldn't even match this number; only 1,256 five-speed plus 4,212 automatic versions of the blown coupes found owners. Base and LX coupes again combined their totals for 59,543 V-6 versions and another 12,562 V-8 copies (including the Sports). Thunderbird's prestige increased on November 10, 1992, when Ford won its 10th NASCAR manufacturer's championship—the first since 1969—due to the Thunderbird-equipped racing teams.

The half-way point for the MN-12 platform theoretically had passed with the 1992 models, but people in Dearborn's planning offices were looking to maximize the mileage they could get from the current body. To reverse the downward trend, as well as hold the line on costs, the number of trim levels for 1993 was reduced to just the LX and the Super Coupe.

Prices were also rolled back, something virtually unheard of since the introduction of the downsized 1977 model. Costing nearly $3,000 less than the previous year's car, the LX managed to retain most of its standard features. The Super Coupe barely dropped its sticker price, holding out at $22,030 for one with no optional equipment. A well-equipped LX would cost about the same.

The LX was still available with either the 3.8-liter V-6 or the 5.0-liter V-8, but it would be the last year that the pushrod workhorse first introduced in 1962 with a 221-ci displacement would be available. The V-8 pumped out 200 ponies at 4,000 revs, with 275 foot-pounds of torque at 3,000 rpm. The Super Coupe made better numbers, with 210 horsepower at 4,000 rpm and 315 foot-pounds of torque at 2,600 rpm. The Windsor small-block was beaten into submission by the supercharged six, but sales figures were the best since 1987. The drop in prices was worth the effort, as a grand total of 130,750 Thunderbirds were turned out, ranking it as the top-selling model year for all MN-12 production.

Things looked good again for the T-Bird, justifying a facelift for 1994 as well as a new mill. Speculation had been raging for some time that the Thunderbird would get the 4.6-liter overhead-cam "Mod-8" engine used in Lincolns and Crown Victorias, including the all-new Mark VIII. The Mod-8 was nothing like the 302/5-liter. It didn't use pushrods to open and close valves, instead relying solely on an overhead camshaft. Late twentieth century technology was prevalent, including remote coil packs, sequential electronic fuel injection, computer controlled operation, and other modern tricks. With fewer cubic centimeters of displacement, the 4.6-liter was able to produce 5 more ponies than the 1993 edition of the 5.0 in dual exhaust configuration (requiring 600 more rpm), but netted less torque at 265 foot-pounds at 3,200 rpm. With the new 4R70W electronic transmission replacing the decade-old AOD, a thoroughly modern driveline was in place. The supercharged V-6 got some refinements as well, such as Teflon-coated rotors, to further quiet their operation.

Cosmetically, the 1994 looked like it developed a case of the mumps or had a lantern jaw. The front fascia caused the overall length of the car to increase 1.6 inches as it

(above) Other than the Super Coupe, the Thunderbird was only available as an LX, such as this 1994 in Moonlight Blue Clearcoat.

(left) The 1992 through 1996 T-Birds with a V-8 were badged for the world to know what was under the hood.

(above) The sole model available for 1996 was the LX. Chrome script on the deck lid is a distinguishing feature for the last of the MN-12s.

(right) The year 1996 marked the T-Bird's 42nd year of continuous production. Silver Blue Mist Metallic Clearcoat was one of 11 colors offered.

bulged out and down to smooth out the front end, with large radiator air inlets flanking the center of the bumper. To aid cooling, a narrow slit with a T-Bird emblem in the center was placed between the headlights, and in turn, the bottom edge of the hood was raised to the midpoint of the polycarbonate headlight lenses. At the bottom of the fascia, air scoops at the outboard ends supplied air for the filter box and intercooler. Around the body, the side moldings were finished in body color and truncated to start at the front of the door, ending just in front of the rear wheel arch. The 16-inch aluminum canted five-spoke wheels were offered on both models, while a new eight-spoke turbine wheel was made available for the LX and included as part of its Preferred Equipment Package in place of the standard vented road wheel covers. If you got the 4.6-liter, you also received V-8 emblems on the front fenders.

Changes to the dash were prevalent. Restyled to be more fluid, the center flowed up and over into the instrument cluster in one swooping gesture. The center console continued the swoop rearward, pulled away from the driver's leg for more room, to swell up and over the storage bin, which contained a pair of cup holders but obscured to the passenger riding shotgun since the console lid hinged on the right side. A set of ducts ran through the console to the rear, feeding conditioned air to back seat occupants. Air bags were now provided in both the steering wheel and behind a panel in front of the front seat passenger. Sadly, color-keyed dashes and steering wheels were now but a distant memory, as insert panels on the driver's door, the dash cluster fascia, center stack, top of console, and glove box lid were now only offered in black. But you could still get a choice of four interior colors for the SC and LX including Opal Grey, Mocha, Portofino Blue, and Ruby Red, as well as an added one for the LX called Evergreen. The cloth seats had a very unique multi-colored pattern, although leather was only available in Opal Gray and Mocha.

The price difference of $1,030 between the V-8 and V-6 versions of the LX was not enough to prevent buyers from selecting more 4.6-liters than 3.8s. Alas, this would be the lowest production year for the Super Coupe, with 2,647 fitted with the new automatic with overdrive lock-out versions, and a paltry 722 with manual shift. This meant that the total number of 1994 Thunderbirds came to 121,082 copies. This wouldn't be the last year that sales would be in six figures, but it would be the last for over 120,000. Thunderbirds won an 11th NASCAR manufacturer's championship for the model year, but it helped 1995s more than 1994s since it was announced in November.

As mid-decade dawned, it appeared more than ever that the sun was setting on the rear-wheel-drive sport coupe. Helping to speed its inevitable demise was the growing popularity of pickup trucks and their more car-like derivative, the sport utility vehicle. With more room and a perception by their buyers that they were safer than the smaller and lighter cars on the road, SUVs exploded in sales to the detriment of other models. The 1995 Thunderbird was in its last year of offering the Super Coupe. The options list's biggest news was deletion of the CD changer in the trunk in favor of an in-dash player that could hold five discs.

Now in its 40th year of continuous production, it was hands-down the longest-lived nameplate in the Ford family, outlasting Fairlane, Galaxie, Falcon, Pinto, Maverick, Fairmont, LTD, Tempo, F-100, and several others. To celebrate, a 40th Anniversary Edition was commissioned to be built outside of the Lorain plant by a subcontractor. Finished Thunderbirds were shipped across town to a conversion facility, where the final transformation took place. Available in all exterior colors, the Anniversary package retailed for an additional $795 over the sticker price. It consisted of a contrasting painted lower body (typically in titanium silver), color-keyed accent tape striping, cloisonné 40th Anniversary Edition emblems on the front fenders and body side trim graphics, embroidered logo floor mats, and a unique key fob. No real promotional effort was expended like in 1990. There was no mention made of it in sales brochures, and little was said about it in the enthusiast press. The only real hype, it seemed, was for 40th Anniversary promotional items like shirts, hats, and posters. It seemed as though the only people who heard or knew about them were either die-hard T-Bird fanatics, or people who simply saw one at a dealership. As a result, only approximately 2,300 of these were spoken for.

Sales dropped again to 115,397 cars. An upsurge in Super Coupe demand, created due to an increase in collectible speculation buying, yielded 5,741 automatic transmission examples. The real collectible may prove to be the five-speed variant because only 574 were produced. This makes it the rarest of Super Coupes. LX numbers totaled 79,721 in both V-6 and V-8 configurations. This would be the last MN-12 with V-8 ornaments.

The marquee of the Boulevard Drive-In reflects off the Laser Red Metallic Clearcoat paint of a 1996 LX. Clearcoat paint became the finishing method of choice by the mid-1990s because it allowed a deep shine with less labor and material.

166 *Chapter Twelve*

A restyled Thunderbird was brought out for 1996. Available for the first time since 1976 as a single model, only the LX was put forward and the Super Coupe was dropped. Distinctions between the six- and the eight-cylinders became more important, but not outwardly visible. A Sport package was assembled to use some of the components left over from the Super Coupe, such as the 16-inch wheels with new center caps that exposed chrome-plated lug nuts. Variable-rate coil springs, larger stabilizer bars, and nitrogen-charged shock absorbers helped to stiffen the chassis' response to the road and improve roadability. And only the V-8 cars would be available with the speed-sensitive variable-assist power rack-and-pinion steering. Strangely, no V-8 badges were used on them, but this also worked to the advantage of those who wanted to surprise the Camaros and GT Mustangs at stoplights. By the end of the model year, an optional rear deck spoiler containing the high-mount third brake light was also available to dress up the tail.

Because dash inserts were only made in black, some owners prefer to go the extra mile to incorporate color to the interior.

The lower body was bulked up with convex plastic overlays, smoothing out the bottom side, and also containing the side molding spears. The spears could be had in body color or contrasting silver inserts both on the body sides and on the front and rear bumper covers. Door handles were now painted body color, rather than the exclusive black used since 1989. The front cover was tweaked to enlarge the upper opening for the radiator, with an updated Thunderbird emblem placed over a honeycombed, black plastic grille. A variation of the grille emblem featured tailfeathers with a pair of turquoise inserts that harkened back to the 1966 and 1969 models. Small oval slots aligned with the body reveal strip, and openings in the bottom fascia took advantage of ground effects to feed air to the radiator and air intake box. Taillights retained the trademark Thunderbird emblems, but lost the black and chrome plastic base strip from previous years' non-SC models. The deck lid now had a cursive script on the driver's side reminiscent of the Thunderbird nameplates of generations before the Aero look, and a small Ford oval on the passenger's side.

The 1996 model looked much better as an overall package than the previous facelift, but the interior was obviously the victim of a move to cut costs in hopes of increasing sales. More plastic was used in place of fabric and vinyl. Only one seat style was offered for front passengers, with color selections in cloth reduced to Portofino Blue, Medium Graphite, Willow Green, and Saddle. Only Portofino Blue was not available in cowhide.

One of the goals of the project team for the Intermediate program was to continue reducing weight and improving fuel economy figures. Prior to the 1996 model year, the intake manifold on the 4.6-liter was an aluminum casting, but for the next generation of the OHC 8, a cast ceramic unit was installed. While it saved weight, it had one drawback—

Mark Martin's No. 6 Valvoline Thunderbird helped Ford earn NASCAR's Manufacturer's Championship for 1997. After the 1997 season, Ford switched to the Taurus platform, even though it didn't offer rear-wheel-drive and two doors in stock form. Courtesy Ivan Veldhuizen/NASCAR Scene

it cracked and leaked. Ford had to develop a replacement aluminum manifold and eat the ceramic ones under warranty.

It looked gloomier for talliers once final results were in. Sales dropped 16,492 for a model year total of 112,302 examples. Sales were still reasonably healthy, but the plug was about to be pulled on Thunderbird's life support.

The 1997 Thunderbird incorporated few changes. Most impressive among these were standard four-wheel disc brakes. Some massaging under the hood also helped to pump up power, with the 3.8 developing 145 whinnies at 4,000 rpm, and 215 foot-pounds at 2,750 rpm, while the 4.6 pulled 205 on the dyno at 4,250 rpm and 280 foot-pounds of torque at 3,000 rpm. For decoration, there were some color changes, such as replacing Saddle with a similar color, Light Prairie Tan. A few new colors were added and some dropped out, but overall there were only 11 to choose from. Courtesy lights in the doors were deleted and replaced by a plastic reflector lens. Pickings had certainly become slim in order to make it more affordable.

One ray of hope for dealers was a Limited Edition package, produced by the same firm that handled the 40th Anniversary Edition. The Limited Edition was a combination of interior and exterior accents, such as embroidered floor mats, reworked cloisonné emblems from the 40th Anniversary car for between the front wheel opening and the door, and silver- or red-colored molding inserts for the sides and bumper covers with "Limited Edition" graphics behind the doors. The package was limited to two interior colors: the new Light Prairie Tan and carried-over Medium Graphite. With a suggested retail price of $239 over the sticker price, it was a feeble attempt to capitalize on collectibility. Other moves would cement the ultimate reason that the Thunderbird would become a true collectible.

Indications that Thunderbird might go into a record-breaking 10th year of production for 1998 were not hidden. Product planners had authorized styling and design to develop prototypes of a 1998 version with a slightly changed front cover and some beefing up of the 4.6-liter. However, in the spring of 1997 management decided to stop Thunderbird and Cougar production at the end of the model year, with the Mark VIII RWD platform ceasing in 1998. Contracts were cancelled, and workers were notified at the Lorain plant that the last job to be scheduled would be completed during the first week of September. Yet, before this happened, there would be some unique T-Birds that would be blocked out for special handling.

As part of a promotion for Valvoline products, the Ashland Corporation arranged to have Jack Roush prepare six Thunderbirds as street-legal clones of the No. 6 car driven in Winston Cup racing by Mark Martin. The half-dozen Birds were painted dark blue to match Martin's Valvoline race car, and provided with gray leather interiors that featured the Valvoline "V" in the headrests, on windows, and other places on the body. Roush's specialists worked over the suspension and drivetrain to give it more oomph than what normally would be produced on an assembly line, and identified each car with a special specification tag. The cars were given away to participants in a late 1997 drawing.

The Thunderbird went out with a bang by claiming its third NASCAR manufacturer's championship and Ford's 12th. However, Ford's backing of Thunderbird racing teams would cease at the end of the 1997 season. The company would throw its support behind the Taurus as the Blue Oval's new Grand National car for 1998, thus ending a memorable and historic run by MN-12 Birds.

The "last" Thunderbird built at Lorain would also receive special handling. During the summer of 1997, Ford contacted all the major national Thunderbird clubs asking if any of them would be willing to be caretakers for the final car, and submit a plan on how they would preserve it. With most clubs lacking the resources to house and maintain the car, the Classic Thunderbird Club International was selected to become the recipient of a Laser Red LX with a 4.6-liter V-8, since it had just purchased a small building to house its operations in Signal Hill, California. Part of the agreement was that both the 1997 and the 005 car owned by former CTCI President George Watts would be stored together to provide a set of "bookends" to the Thunderbird line. The work order was drawn up, and even though it would carry a lower serial number than even the Valvoline Thunderbirds, the standing order was that this would be the official "last" car.

(above) Among the last of the 1997 T-Birds to be built was this LX, one of six given away in a promotion by Valvoline Motor Oil late in the year.

(right) The dash plaque identifies the car as one of the Mark Martin signature edition Roush-modified cars.

On Friday, September 9, 1997, a subdued ceremony was held at the end of the Final Acceptance and Delivery area at Lorain. A few days before, workers in the body assembly area stamped out a metal "buck" tag that was coded with items to be installed on one of the bodies being welded together. Unique about the tag designated for the body to be assigned consecutive unit number 173196 was the bottom line, which read "LORAIN ASSY LAST T BIRD." With no other cars following it out of the inspection area, plant operations moved from assembly to demobilization and change-over for other products. Outside the plant, workers and enthusiasts carried a mock coffin and proceeded from the plant for their own wake.

Outfitted with a spoiler on the rear deck and chrome 15-inch uni-directional wheels, the car was rolled out for final inspection, then loaded onto a transporter for delivery to its new home in southern California. Once the 2002 Thunderbird started reaching production, the Board of Directors of CTCI decided to dispose of the car by auctioning it off to its membership. The winning bidder trucked the historic "last of the breed" off to a new home.

As the sun set on 43 years of continuous production, one nagging question was how could the nameplate be allowed to die such an ignoble death? The answer was that it wasn't dead—it was going into hibernation until a worthy successor could be developed. Nobody, outside of a select few, had any idea that within a few years the Thunderbird would fly again.

(below) The 1997 Mark Martin Signature Edition Valvoline T-Birds were fitted with custom wheels, rear deck spoiler, and the Valvoline logo in various places around the car and inside.

CHAPTER THIRTEEN

2002-2005
Resurrection

The first 200 of the new T-birds were Neiman-Marcus editions with their black bodies and silver hardtops. All were ordered within a 2 hour and 15 minute period.

(opposite) Thunderbird emblems of the past were studied extensively before the final version for the 2002 series, with its narrow wings and turquoise inserts, was chosen.

It appeared that the Thunderbird's wings had been clipped. After a record setting run of 43 years in continuous production, it was over. The car that reinvented itself as it needed to wasn't being brought back to finish out the millennium. Or, was that what you were supposed to think? The people who controlled the Thunderbird's destiny had an idea, but it needed time to gel.

The Thunderbird name is as magical as it is emotional for many who bleed Ford blue. It survived periods of crisis, was tweaked and adapted for the times it was meant to service, and became more than mere transportation for many people not only in the United States, but virtually the entire world. Mention the word to anyone on the Ginza, Kurfurstendamm, the Spanish Steps, Champs-Elysées, or Piccadilly Circus, and it will invoke images of that little two-seat jewel that became an icon alongside the gull-wing Mercedes 300s and Jaguar XKEs. No, the nameplate wasn't dead, just dormant, waiting for the right time to be hatched anew and brought back into the public eye.

Through the mid to late 1990s, other manufacturers turned out cars such as the Plymouth Prowler, PT Cruiser, and the Bug with a nostalgic flavor they thought the public was yearning for. Retro-styling struck a chord with older generations who had fond memories of their parents' sedans or uncles' hot rods, and even the lowly hulks that took them across campus when in high school and college. The retro-look was hot, and opportunity was knocking on the door at Ford's Design Center.

Internally, the decision to nix the MN-12 had been anticipated in the mid-1990s when sales figures began to tank. Ford leadership had determined that rear-wheel drive platforms were not high on consumers' wish lists for cars, with the exception of the Crown Victoria/Grand Marquis and Lincoln Town Cars. To maintain profitability, Ford had to revamp or terminate under-performing lines. Management's announcement that this would include the company's first minivan, the Aerostar, along with other RWD platforms including Lincoln Mark VIII and the Cougar/Thunderbird, was not so much a shock as a recognition that time was marching on.

Still, there were some within the organization who couldn't bear to see the Bird's wings folded up. As it happened in the early 1950s, a small group of people initiated a covert effort to develop a new rendition of an image car. Well before the end of 1997 production, dedicated individuals had sketches and cost studies well under way, oftentimes without budgeting or official approval. Some of the team spent their free time on this labor of love without a thought that it would not be accepted. Ted Finney, head designer of large and luxury cars under Dave Turner—who was director of the rear-wheel-drive division—began to enlist the help of others to move the project forward with assistance from product planner Rich Kisler and engineer, Don Warneke. History's repetition of the scenario with Hershey, Boyer, and Case was well under way.

Jack Telnack, the person named responsible for the 1980s AeroBird as well as the Taurus, was poised to retire as vice president of Styling upon completion of such cars as the 1998 Cougar, the two-door, two-seat coupe that brought Mercury a halo car of its own. His

The DEW-98 platform for Lincoln's LS was the basis for the 2002 T-Bird. Both cars are built at the same assembly plant in Wixom, Michigan, and share many components. Alan H. Tast

thoughts were the same: the Thunderbird couldn't be allowed to die. Tacit approval was given for various studios to come up with their own renditions of what a 2000 Thunderbird should look like. Not only would the Rear Wheel Drive studio develop concepts: the Front Wheel Drive studio, Pacific Design Center in California, the Ghia studio in Italy, and Ford's German design studios were all given the package information needed to develop proposals based on an in-production platform. By the spring of 1997, these studios were quietly sneaking fiberglass mock-ups to Dearborn for evaluation.

In the end, the most captivating design would be the Rear Wheel Drive studio's rendition of a two-seater with the Classic 'Bird's reverse-wedge styling cues. To help stylists and designers understand what a classic Thunderbird was about, Turner secured approval to purchase both an original 1955 and 1957 for use in the studio. People not old enough to have been born when the cars were approaching their 25th anniversary needed to become familiar with them and understand the styling that had made them icons.

One of the major supporters for a two-seat Thunderbird was Ford's new president, Jacques "Jac" Nasser, an import from Ford's European operations. Jac became aware of the surreptitious project only after the team's players had put their entire package together, including all-important cost information. Like the first-generation car, building it meant

(above) Desert Sky Blue was a 2003-only color for the Thunderbird. Reverse wedge styling gives the car a sporty rake.

(right) Complaints about the difficulty in using and storing a hard cover for the convertible top led to the introduction of a soft cover for 2003.

relying on components from other Ford products. When Nasser asked if it could utilize Lincoln's new DEW-98 platform for a rear-wheel-drive intermediate-size sedan, then on the drawing boards, it was virtually impossible to say no without killing the program. From that point on, Nasser was a staunch proponent of the new coupe, and much like his predecessors McNamara, Iacocca, and Knudsen, Jac exercised executive privilege with its design, demanding that it have round taillights as one of its styling cues.

In the fall of 1997, Telnack received his gold watch after working on Ford products from the early Thunderbirds and first-generation Mustang through the new two-seat Cougar. To replace him, Ford hired the young designer who had made a rolling statement with the reincarnation of the Volkswagen Beetle, a styling consultant by the name of J. Mays. The melding of nostalgic styling with modern technology made the 1990s version of the People's Car a breakout platform for Mays, a stylist with a knack for what was rapidly becoming known as retro-design. Mays was aware that there was a two-seat Thunderbird program underway, and even saw the design competition mock-ups in mid-1997.

Mays quickly became involved with the now-official Thunderbird program and began to wield his influence. Having seen the competition studies from earlier in the year, he began to take a look at what had transpired since then. At about the same time, following Finney and Turner's retirements and prior to his own, Telnack passed the torch for the Thunderbird's development to Doug Gaffka. By this point, some of the studies had busy front ends with silver plastic bumpers or heavy-handed rear lights as requested by Nasser. Leaving Gaffka to continue resolving issues with the car's evolution, Mays started adding his comments and direction until the form recognizable as the new Thunderbird came into focus by the summer of 1998.

Visual cues were important to carry forward the retro-look, but they couldn't be so overdone that they killed the difference between subtle and obvious. Bumper fascias were formed to flow and wrap around rather than have a character of their own, with a concession to mimic the 1955–1956 Dagmars by surrounding a pair of driving lights. Headlights were made rounder, pulled backward, and thankfully weren't given an eyebrow-like hood. A large, vacuum-plated plastic grille with a heavy egg-crate grid gaped open from the center and flushed out with the body. An interpretation of the "power dome" was pulled off by slightly raising the center enough around and behind a simulated intake to provide a bulge, while forward of the trademark scoop, the hood was dished out for a modern flair.

The proportions of the body side were set up similar to an early 1960s Thunderbird with the door centered between the wheel arches, with an upper body feature line running from a faux opening with hints of the first generation's hash marks. To position the door where it needed to be, engineers had to develop the body structure and extend the cowl sidewalls back in order to mount the hinges. Engineers also took great pride in developing the windshield so that it could visually capture the wrap-around feel of the 1960s-era cars. By incorporating a 64-degree slant to the A-pillars and utilizing a mold process to form the compound-curved sandwich of glass and plastic safety film, the designers moved the dashboard forward over the cowl.

Taillights protruded from the top of the rear fender, but were recessed into the bumper cover, helping reestablish the twin-pontoon look that was a T-Bird trademark through the early 1980s. Twin exhaust tips exited under the fascia in cut-outs at the bottom edge. A rounded trapezoid, reminiscent of a large exhaust port, was framed in chrome and housed the recessed license plate.

Ornamentation was simple, elegant, and true to the Thunderbird heritage. At the rear below the feature line and forward of the taillights, the Thunderbird script similar to 1957 and 1961-1962 was adapted and refined for an updated look. Emblems on the nose, rear deck lid, steering wheel center cover, and instrument panel pulled together a wide-wingspan motif using a turquoise center bar flanked by chromed leading and trailing edges with a center body reminiscent of the 1964-style version. Even the door panels got the Thunderbird touch with the armrest and brushed metal trim shaped to look like a bird's wing, especially visible when the doors are opened and viewed from the rear. To put anything else on would be overkill.

One original touch designers would repeat was the totally hidden convertible top. People wanted to be able to push a button and let the top up automatically, but not at the sacrifice of trunk room or the inconvenience of having to get out of their seats and manipulate the hardware. This meant that a traditional top well and boot to cover the folded-up assembly would be needed. This also allowed for the rear light to be made of glass and incorporate heating elements for a defroster. A hardshell fold-over cover was developed that could be stowed in the trunk, but its bulky design received low grades from owners once it reached production. A dealer-optional fabric cover was offered to satisfy those who preferred to roll it up and use less space.

There would also be a return to the removable fiberglass porthole hardtop, one of the key features that says "Thunderbird" in any language. Given a sharp feature line for the transition from horizontal to vertical, its rounded edge for the door glass gave another salute back to its forebear. However, as with the 1955–1957s before it, the weather stripping along the top's bottom edge created a noticeable rim of discoloration as the top moved on the body. The resulting scratches and damaged paint led option engineers to experiment with self-adhesive mylar strips that could isolate the rubber from the enamel. Owners were instructed to remove the strips when they took the hardtop off, but once removed, they had to fit a new one, at a cost of about $13 per set from the dealer. Ford tried a permanent solution with a polished stainless-steel trim strip on pre-production 2003s, but it also suffered from scratches and rubber scuffs. Some people argued that a brushed finish, as used on the dash panels, would have done the trick. Aftermarket vendors eventually picked up the ball and offered the metal rub strips.

The DEW-98 platform also shared suspension components and the instrument panel with the T-Bird. The practical move for Ford was to restore T-Bird production to the Wixom Assembly Plant, which had sent its last Thunderbird rolling out the north doors in July

1976. The new Thunderbird would share plant space with the Lincoln Town Car and the other recipients of the DEW-98 architecture, the baby Lincoln LS.

Like the 1997, it has variable-ratio rack-and-pinion steering, four-wheel disc brakes, and independent rear suspension, but the similarities end there. New 17-inch diameter cast aluminum wheels would be offered with a 21-spoke design, patterned to use seven sets of two narrow blades radiating from the center hub to the outside edge of the rim with a wider third spoke in the center. Painted silver in production form, it was much finer in detail than the optional chrome-plated, seven-spoke design available for the premium model. The disintegration of Ford's relationship with Firestone (which dated back to the very beginnings of both companies and the relationship of Henry Ford and Harvey Firestone) over the failures of the Wilderness AT radial tires used on Explorers played a significant role in the car's development. Although pre-production cars were spotted with 235/50R17 Firestone Firehawk performance radials, production variants used Michelins exclusively. Tread widths with the wide meats of 60.5 inches in the front and 60.2 inches in the rear exceeded the 1955–1957s by well over four inches.

Now set on a 107.2-inch wheelbase, in contrast to the LS' 114.5 inches and the original car's 102, the car had proportions more in line with the first generation. The overall body length of 186.3 inches and width of 6 feet was greater than any of the original Little Birds (the 1957 was 181.4 inches by 71 inches). At a height of 52.1 inches, it was under the height of the 1955–1956 by only a tenth of an inch. Curb weight would vary from 3,775 pounds without a top in Deluxe trim to 3,869 pounds with the top and the premium package.

A supercharger-equipped concept car was displayed for the 2003 auto show circuit and took center stage in Ford's Living Legends tent at its 100th Anniversary celebration in Dearborn. Tim Pundt

Since it would be a smaller car, the designers didn't pursue a large engine, but it definitely had to have a V-8 to be worthy of the Thunderbird name. Instead of continuing with the 4.6-liter, Thunderbird would utilize the LS-8's 3.9-liter dual overhead cam version with a cast aluminum block and cylinder heads, four-valves-per-cylinder, sequential electronic fuel injection, and a five-speed automatic transmission with overdrive. The new engine offered 252 horsepower at a high-revving 6,100 rpm, and 261 foot-pounds of twist at 4,300 spins per minute. The arrangement of the engine

The Saleen Bon Speed T-Bird was conceived as a high-horsepower, limited-production T-Bird to be marketed through Ford dealers. Tim Pundt

bay left little room for items like the battery. Taking a cue from cars like the Boss 429, designers moved the battery below the trunk floor, where it helped balance out front-rear weight distribution. The engine itself was covered with a large, formed plastic shroud, revealing very little underneath. The Bird for the twenty-first century certainly would sound, as well as drive, differently.

Barely a year after the lights were turned out in Lorain and the brochures pulled out of Ford dealers' racks, rumors were starting to circulate that there was something afoot in the building complex across the road from Greenfield Village. Sketches were appearing in trade journals such as Automotive News by mid-May showing a new concept two-seat Ford with styling cues aimed backward at least 45 years. This could only mean one thing: Thunderbird was coming back for the new millennium as the car people had been screaming for since December 1957.

As the fall of 1998 progressed into December, the rumors became the truth. The beginning of 1999 would be dramatic, as Ford chairman Sir Alex Troutman retired and was succeeded by William Clay Ford, Jr., as chairman, and Nasser assumed the presidency and chief executive officer position. Amid fanfare at the 1999 Detroit Auto Show, Ford put a bright Goldenrod Yellow coupe with two seats, an egg-crate grille, removable roof, and portholes on display for the automotive press and public on January 3, 1999. The car was subsequently taken on tour around the country, along with a Torch Red sister, as well as exhibited in Europe at the Geneva International Auto Show beginning on March 9, to gauge public reaction. Thunderbird fans didn't know what to think. In front of them, for the first time in nearly five decades, was the answer to their collective prayers—a brand-new two-seater that could claim to be a direct descendant of the work started back in 1953. From the standpoint of development, it almost really was late February 1954 all over again.

It was a "love it/hate it" affair with die-hard classic fans. Some bemoaned the "melted jellybean/pug nose" look and compared it to a Mazda Miata with a thyroid condition. Others felt it should have a totally retro-inspired look down to the recessed grille, tailfins, and hooded headlights. Some even wanted to see a continental kit as standard equipment. Quipped designer Gaffka, "If they want all that, they should buy an original." Ford did do some tweaking in response to public reactions. The most noticeable change was that drip rails, missing from the concept car hardtops, were installed and trimmed in stainless steel. When compared with competitors, BMW's Z3 Roadster and Porsche's Boxster, Ford stressed "relaxed sportiness" to distance the T-Bird from the Teutonic bahn-burners.

The announcement that everyone had waited for was finally made in the summer of 2000. Ford management gave the go-ahead to begin production with deliveries to dealers starting in summer 2001. To help pump up initial demand for the car, marketing made arrangements with upscale retailer Neiman-Marcus to sell the first 200 cars. For their Christmas 2000 catalog, the retailer would offer new Thunderbirds with a black body, silver hardtop, and black interior with silver leather inserts, a gray-colored lower dash and armrest fairings. A Neiman-Marcus insignia was placed on the brushed aluminum dash panel over the glove box and engraved into the portholes. To complete the exterior, a chromed hood scoop casting and chrome-plated versions of the standard 21-spoke road wheels were placed over the hubs. The allotment of limited-edition drop-tops was spoken for within a period of two-and-a-quarter hours on September 26, 2000, at a price of $41,995 a copy. Others wanting a new Thunderbird would have to go to their local Ford dealer, place a deposit, and wait for Wixom to start churning out new Birds in the summer of 2001.

By design, Ford kept color and trim choices limited. Planners decided that in order to create an immediate collector appeal, certain colors would only be offered for each model year. Among the first limited-edition colors were two tied to the 1955: Thunderbird Blue Metallic and Inspiration Yellow paid homage to Thunderbird Blue/Skyhaze Green and Goldenrod Yellow. Whisper White, Torch Red (another throwback to the first generation), and Evening Black would be offered for the body, while for the removable hardtop either the body color or a brighter Performance White was used. As cars were delivered, it wasn't uncommon for top colors to be mixed and matched by dealers to satisfy owner preferences. The convertible top, though, was only available in a black fabric. And what of the attractive chrome-plated scoop used on the Neiman-Marcus cars? It wasn't available in production, but you could order one from the parts counter and swap it out.

Inside, everything in leather, vinyl, or plastic was black unless the buyer opted for the Partial Accent or Full Color Accent package. The Partial Color Accent Package featured either red, yellow, or aqua leather seat inserts to match the exterior colors, with a high-gloss application on the upper portion of the steering wheel and shift knob. The Full Color Accent group added the same colors to the lower console, door trim panels, and lower dash board. Another option was the Black Accent Package, which applied the high-gloss treatment to the upper steering wheel and shift knob of the Midnight Black interior.

Confusing prospective buyers, the car was offered with or without the hardtop in two levels, deluxe and premium. When the hardtop was ordered, more items were made available for the lower-end deluxe buyer than just driving lights (which could not be provided on Canadian-exported units) and the black interior accent package. The deluxe model, which originally retailed for $35,390 without the hardtop and $38,890 with, was already pretty well endowed. Niceties like the Audiophile sound system and six CD changer stereo, automatic headlights, air conditioning with individual controls for the driver and passenger, power windows/locks/mirrors, powered six-way driver's and two-way passenger seats, and the powered convertible top with heated back glass gave it a solid list of features. The removable hardtop came standard with heated back glass, a storage cart, and vinyl cover.

Unlike the movie version, the 2003 "007" Editions had a Performance White hardtop over the Coral body.

Premium level buyers could have all-speed traction control and the seven-spoke chrome wheels, along with the colored accent packages. However, Canadian buyers again were shortchanged; only the deluxe painted wheels would be sent over the Ambassador Bridge for distribution in the Commonwealth (reportedly due to a shortage of chrome wheels for U.S. buyers), but they did get a block heater and automatic traction control as standard equipment. Premium models' suggested prices were $36,960 without and $37,890 with the hardtop.

Pent-up demand for the Retrobird took on a life of its own. Dealers began taking orders over a year and a half before initial deliveries began, while the suggested retail prices rose to $35,495 for a soft-top-only Deluxe and $40,245 for a loaded Premium model. Imposing surcharges on the suggested list price—some hiking the cost of buying a new one to nearly $50,000—was a problem nationwide as well, recalling the feeding frenzy that accompanied introduction of the 1991 Miata, and later the Beetle and PT Cruiser. The property was hot! Production commenced on June 5, 2001, and once the cars started flowing into dealer showrooms in the late summer of 2001, people willingly paid premium money for the chance to be among the first to own the new classic. Even early problems such as a hold on release of the first few thousand cars due to quality problems with a malfunctioning hydraulic cooling fan motor. Then the tragedy on September 11, 2001, shook the nation, and suddenly a new car model seemed distant and unimportant. Shortly thereafter, Thunderbird champion Jac Nasser, after struggling to share power with Bill Ford, was shown the door on October 30.

A far cry from the chromed dress-up kits of the 1950s, today's T-Birds are literally hidden under a plastic cover.

Despite turmoil within and outside of Ford, the new T-Bird's introductory year brought it critical praise and honors. *Motor Trend* named Thunderbird its "Car of the Year" for the fourth time in its history (following 1958, 1987, and 1989), a record for one badge. Other awards followed, including Motor Week's choice as "Best Convertible" for 2002.

Demand for the new Thunderbird was not initially quelled, but as the year ended and 2002 progressed, the sales curve began to dip. Marketing projected 25,000 annual sales for at least four model years, but growing dissatisfaction with dealer inflation of the sticker price had an adverse effect on buyers. Sales dropped off after those who really wanted one got their hands on them, but production continued unabated. As the new model introduction time for 2003 came and went, Wixom was still putting together the prior edition through November 14, resulting in 31,121 cars being titled as 2002s. Of the 2002s, 280 deluxes and 1,686 premiums were sans hardtop, while there were 2,785 deluxes and 26,170 delivered with the hardtop, not including the 200 Neiman-Marcus examples.

The 2003 edition was not a radically changed successor to the 2002, but there were improvements. The biggest upgrade was the engine, which could now pump out 280 horses at 6,000 revs and 286 foot-pounds at 4,000 rpm. The additional 28 horsepower and 19 foot-pounds with fewer rotations than the previous iteration was due in part to a 10.75-to-1 compression ratio engine that used premium unleaded fuel. This was accomplished with variable cam timing and electronic throttle control. Buyers also got a second choice of automatics in the SelectShift, which allowed the driver to work through the five forward speeds manually without a clutch, for 17 miles per gallon in the city and 23 miles per gallon on the open highway. All-Speed Traction Control also became a regular feature on all cars, regardless of whether it was a deluxe or premium type. The premium package did get an added standard feature of heated driver and passenger seats, along with the chrome seven-spoke wheels. Instruments were also revised so that the Lincoln LS's distinct overlapping tachometer and speedometer were now separate dials, with 7,000 rpm, 160 mile per hour limits.

T-Bird Blue and Inspiration Yellow dropped from the fashion colors palette, were replaced by a dark, metallic Mountain Shadow Grey and a pastel-like Desert Sky Blue. Evening Black, Torch Red, and Whisper White remained in the brochure, along with the Performance White hardtop for non-white bodied cars. Torch Red would prove the most popular, followed by Grey; Desert Sky Blue was the least-liked of the choices. The Black (charcoal) interior was renamed Black Ink, color accent packages added Saddle when used with the black or grey exterior with a unique colored steering wheel rim, while white was added to the partial interior accent group for the seat inserts, upper steering wheel rim, and shifter knob. Exterior trim was slightly altered with painted drip rails on the hardtops and a V-8 badge on the front fenders just forward of the doors. The hardtop was not immune, at least 13 improvements were made to it over the 2002s.

Mint Green was only offered on early 2004 models through December 2003.

If the Neiman-Marcus edition was the collector's car for 2002, the ultimate collectible 2003 had a movie tie-in. In an arrangement with producers of the James Bond films, Ford supplied a variety of its vehicles for use in *Die Another Day*, including a coral-colored 2002 Thunderbird driven by Bond's CIA counterpart, Jinx, played by Halle Berry. Ford developed a public 007 Edition in the same Coral color, but with a Performance White hardtop. Spin-ray texturing was used on the passenger side. A serialized number plate was riveted to the body in the glove compartment. Of the 700 007 units produced between December 2002 and

March 2003, 694 were actually sold to the public for a sticker price of $43,995 per copy, while six were retained for use on the auto show circuit. When offered one of the coral cars for her work on the film, Berry instead chose an Evening Black car with hardtop.

Ford had another reason to celebrate in 2003—it was the company's 100th Anniversary, culminating in a five-day celebration at the Henry Ford II World Headquarters complex in Dearborn. Over 250,000 people paid homage and viewed over 3,000 examples of original, restored, and modified Ford products from around the globe representing the company's past, present, and future. In the same tent with the new Ford GT was an interesting concept car, a supercharged silver Thunderbird with a tan leather interior. The blown Bird with its vented hood and throwback Ford-lettered center caps was a teaser for those wanting the T-Bird to max out the potential of the 3.9-liter V-8. However, the idea of a SuperBird did not get enough support for production. A prototype with a supercharged R engine was also built but rejected. Stranger yet, Ford did not produce a Centennial Edition Thunderbird, even though there were versions of these in an F-150 Crew Cab, Taurus SEL, Explorer, Mustang GT, and Focus ZTS.

There was interest from outside of Ford for a supercharged version. Steve Saleen's operation actively worked to produce prototypes of the BonSpeed Thunderbird, which had a restyled rear deck lid, Sports-Roadsteresque tonneau cover, horizontal-barred billet aluminum grille, and chin spoiler/ground effects. Promoted to those who also sold Saleen Mustangs, the supercharged Bird appeared imminent through the winter of 2003-2004, but the effort was axed after the beginning of the year.

The extended run of 2002 production led to a shortened 9-month run for 2003. Production levels dropped enough to warrant reducing the number of shifts at Wixom from two to one, and line output was slowed to a rate of approximately six cars per hour. Even though retail prices were increased to $36,340 for a deluxe without a hardtop and

The V-8 emblem for 2004 was supposed to be placed in the upper front fender cutouts, but it was kept in its originally location. Wheel center caps hearken back to 1957's turbine covers.

The trademark Thunderbird script was brought back for 2002 and subsequent editions as another link to the car's storied past.

$38,840 with it, or $37,385 for a premium without and $39,885 with it, Ford was offering incentives to dealers to move cars with discount rates that often weren't known about by consumers. By the time reports were filed for the period beginning in December 2002 and ending June 27, production volume was less than that for any of the Little Birds, at 14,506 cars. Of these, 700 were Deluxes without hardtops, while 691 Deluxes had them. By far the Premium model with hardtop took the lion's share of sales with 11,574 examples. Only Premium editions were exported to Canada.

As the euphoria of the 100th Anniversary celebration faded away, new model introductions for 2004 took on new significance. Ford was gearing up for release of a host of new models for 2005, and so things quieted down. Thunderbird received an infusion of changes to increase its market appeal. Among these was a new 16-spoke painted cast aluminum wheel for the Deluxe, using the same white-background centers as the Supercharger concept car. The same wheel was optional on the Premium version with micro-machined spokes, while the chrome seven-spoke used the past few years was now modified to have center veins machined into it. The 2003s brushed aluminum trim with a grid pattern was replaced with a horizontal ribbed pattern. The map light was moved from the rearview mirror to the windshield header. Plans for incorporating the V-8 emblem in the fender chevrons were dropped at the last minute due to quality problems.

Fashion colors were subjected to another round of changes, as were the standard ones. Whisper White was dropped and replaced by Platinum Silver, while a dark burgundy, Merlot, and Vintage Mint Green became 2004-only selections; Vintage Mint Green was only available through the end of December 2003. Interior color was limited to black with optional accents in red and white. Upholstery patterns changed from horizontal to vertical pleats. A new Light Sand Appearance Package, adding $1,000 to the base price, was a modification of the other appearance groups incorporating the accent color around the entire steering wheel rim, as well as for the convertible top and optional soft top boot. The dash and shifter accent panels were also finished differently, using bronze-tinted aluminum. Two-speed variable interval wipers, changed from the speed-sensitive version used in 2002, added a heated park function. Ford also made mid-year changes. Ice Blue Metallic replaced Vintage Mint Green as a fashion color in

January, while a Merlot convertible top was added to the black and Merlot-colored exterior/interior combinations.

The deluxe version with hardtop was dropped from the model list—those who wanted the base-model Thunderbird would have to spend an additional $2,500 to get the hard shell. Pricing started at $36,925 for the deluxe without hardtop, but by mid-year had risen to $37,049, while the premium variant without hardtop commanded $38,090. Weights ranged from 3,775 pounds for a deluxe without a hardtop to 3,876 pounds for a fully loaded premium model.

As the year's special edition model, the Pacific Coast Roadster was released in December 2003. The Pacific Coast Roadster used a Lincoln LS color, Light Tundra Metallic, and combined it with a unique Light/Dark Ash Premium-pattern interior, cream-colored instruments, dot-pattern dash/door trim, and serial-numbered identification plates. Limited to 1,000 copies, the model retailed for $43,995.

As 2004 production began on July 14, 2003, reports of poor sales for Thunderbird were fueling rumors that production would cease as early as the end of the current model year, or maybe continue through 2005 for the T-Bird's 50th Anniversary. In late January 2004, United Auto Workers Local 36 agreed to a contract that guaranteed production of the Thunderbird at Wixom through 2006. Enthusiast websites speculated that this was done to keep production tooling in place for the anticipated Lincoln Mark X, debuted at the 2004 Detroit Auto Show and slated for debut in 2007 on a modified Thunderbird platform with a retractable hardtop similar to Mercedes' and Lexus' drop-tops. The agreement also provided that the plant would be reorganized so that the Thunderbird shared the same assembly lines with the Lincoln LS models instead of being segregated as it had been since starting up in 2001. By February, the separate trim line on the second floor of Wixom and the final assembly area on the east end of the plant were integrated into combined LS/T-Bird production, recalling days of old when Lincolns and Thunderbirds shared the same conveyor lines. The company also set up Ford GT production at Wixom, assuring even more attention for the plant. By the end of the model year's production run, approximately 12,900 cars were built with Merlot being the most-popular color.

For 2005, Ford will have a special 50th Anniversary Edition for the year's limited edition feature car in gold with a black and gold interior, plus gold hardtops and soft tops. Other changes are deletion of the Merlot, Vintage Mint Green, and Light Ice Blue exterior, and the addition of Medium Steel Blue and Bronze at the beginning of the year. Other colors will come mid-year. For the interior, color selections are Black with either Medium Steel Blue or Light Sand accents. Soft tops include Medium Steel Blue, Black, and Light Sand to coordinate with interior/exterior colors. A distinguishing feature for all 2005 models will be 50th Anniversary emblems on both front fenders, and pyramid-style texturing for interior aluminum trim.

The Retrobird provides a perfect bookend for 50 iconic years. Whether Ford will extend the model to future designs depends on market whims, corporate priorities, and the not-too-discounted loyalty of the men and women who create, build, and cherish one of the auto industry's most widely recognized accomplishments.

Appendix

THUNDERBIRD PRODUCTION—1955–2005
Detailed breakdowns of production, including engine and drivetrain installations, may include estimates based upon data available to the Author at the time of publication. No guarantees are given for the accuracy of figures presented.

1955
P 292-ci V-8 convertible 16,155
Total 16,155

1956
M 292-ci V-8 convertible
P 312-ci V-8 convertible
Total 15,631

1957
C 292-ci V-8 convertible 3,247
D 312-ci V-8 convertible 16,423
E 312-ci V-8 convertible
(incl. race version) 1,499
F 312-ci supercharged V-8 convertible
(incl. D/F) 211
Total 21,380
w/ automatic transmission 19,242
w/ three-speed manual transmission 1,286
w/ overdrive transmission 757
1955–1957 sources: *Automotive News* annual statistical issues, *Automotive Industries*, and *The Early Bird* by Classic Thunderbird Club International.

1958
H 352-ci hardtop 35,758
H 352-ci convertible 2,134
Total 37,892
w/ automatic transmission 37,034*
w/ three-speed manual transmission 379*
w/ overdrive transmission 379*
*Estimate based on 1959–1960 percentages provided in *Automotive Industries* 1961 statistical issue.

1959
H 352-ci hardtop 54,041
J 430-ci hardtop 3,154
H 352-ci convertible 9,093
J 430-ci convertible 1,168
Total 67,456
w/ automatic transmission 66,107*
w/ three-speed manual transmission 675*
w/ overdrive transmission 675*
*Estimate based on 1959–1960 percentages provided in *Automotive Industries* 1961 statistical issue. Although the 430-ci engine option was not officially available with a manual transmission, at least one convertible has been documented with a factory installation, most likely a one-off by special order.

1960
Y 352-ci hardtop 74,547
J 430-ci hardtop 3,900
Y 352-ci sunroof 2,159
J 430-ci sunroof 377
Y 352-ci convertible 10,606
J 430-ci convertible 1,254
Total 92,843
w/ automatic transmission 90,986*
w/ three-speed manual transmission 928*
w/ overdrive transmission 928*
*Estimate based on 1959–1960 percentages provided in *Automotive Industries* 1961 statistical issue.

1961
Hardtop 62,535
Convertible 10,516
Total 73,051

1962+
Hardtop 68,127
Landau . . . .(Included w/ hardtops)
Convertible 8,457
Sports Roadster 1419*
Total 78,011
No separate production totals were kept for the 1962 Landau; their numbers are included in the hardtop figure. Up to 15 percent may be Landaus.

*Sports Roadster production may have been 1,420 total, with 129 having the M-series engine, according to a revised count of invoices compiled by the Thunderbird Sports Roadster Society newsletter dated March 1, 1976.

+Optional Engines: 120 Sports Roadsters are confirmed by invoices to have been built. No production data survives to break out M-, R-, or Z-engine hardtops/Landaus. From data compiled by *VTCI* and William Wonder, as of January 1, 2004, the following are accounted for with the M- and R-series engines. It is highly likely that more exist that have not been documented.
M 390-ci V-8 6v Hardtop 34
M 390-ci V-8 6v Landau 12
M 390-ciV-8 6v Convertible 17
M 390-ci V-8 6v Sports Roadster* 120
R 390-ci V-8 4v–Low Compression
Sports Roadster* 8

1963+
Hardtop 42,806
Landau 12,139
Limited Edition Monaco Landau 2,000
Convertible 5913
Sports Roadster .455*
Total 63,313
*Sports Roadster production may have been 460 total, with 39 having the M-series engine, according to a revised count of invoices compiled by the Thunderbird Bird Sports Roadster Society in a newsletter dated March 1, 1976.

+Optional Engines: 37 Sports Roadsters are confirmed by invoices. No production data survives to break out M-, 9-, or Z-engine Hardtops/Landaus. From data compiled by *VTCI* and William Wonder, as of January 1, 2004, the following are accounted for with the M- and 9-series engines. It is highly likely that more exist that have not been documented.
M 390-ci V-8 6v Hardtop 27
M 390-ci V-8 6v Landau 22
M 390-ci V-8 6v Convertible 28
M 390-ci V-8 6v Sports Roadster* 37
9 390-ci V-8 4v–Low Compression
Sports Roadster* 7
Total 121

1964
Hardtop 60,552
Landau 22,715
Convertible* 9,198
Total 92,465
*No Sports Roadster was offered in 1964. However, 45 convertibles were supplied from the Wixom plant with both wire wheels and the Sports Tonneau cover.

1965
Hardtop 42,652
Landau 20,974
Special Landau* 4,500
Convertible 6,846
Total 74,972
*Of the 4,500 Special Landaus, an estimated 10 percent (450 +/-) were painted Wimbledon White. More research is required to verify this figure.

1966+
Hardtop 13,389
Town Hardtop .15,633
Town Landau 35,105
Convertible 5,049
Total 69,176
+No separate records were kept for Q-engine 428-ci 1966 T-birds. It is estimated, based on data collected by the author from *VTCI Owners Surveys* and other sources, that between 20–25 percent may have been built with the motor. More research is required to verify this estimate.

1958–1966 Sources: *Automotive News* annual statistical issues, *Automotive Industries*, and *Thunderbird Scoop* by Vintage Thunderbird Club International.

1967
Hardtop 15,567
Landau 37,442
Four-Door Landau 24,967
Total **77,976**
No separate records were kept for Q-engine 428-ci 1967 T-Birds.

1968
Hardtop w/ bucket seats 5,420
Hardtop w/ bench seat 4,557
Landau w/ bucket seats 19,105
Landau w/ bench seat 13,924
Four-Door Landau w/ bucket seats 4,674
Four-Door Landau w/ bench seat 17,251
Total **64,931**
No separate records were kept for Z-engine 390-ci 1968 T-Birds.

1969
Hardtop w/ bucket seats 2,361
Hardtop w/ bench seat 3,552
Landau w/ bucket seats 12,425
Landau w/ bench seat 15,239
Four-Door Landau w/ bucket seats 1,983
Four-Door Landau w/ bench seat 13,712
Total **49,272**
No separate records were kept for sunroof-equipped T-Birds.

1970
Hardtop w/ bucket seats 1,925
Hardtop w/ bench seat 3,191
Landau w/ bucket seats 16,953
Landau w/ bench seat 19,894
Four-Door Landau w/ bucket seats 5,005
Four-Door Landau w/ bench seat 3,396
Total **50,364**
No separate records for Brougham-option or for sunroof-equipped T-Birds.

1971
Hardtop w/ bucket seats 2,992
Hardtop w/ bench seat 6,154
Landau w/ bucket seats 8,133
Landau w/ bench seat 12,223
Four-Door Landau w/ split bench seats ... 4,238
Four-Door Landau w/ bench seat 2,315
Total **36,055**
No separate records for Brougham-option or for sunroof-equipped T-Birds.
1967–1971 Sources: *Automotive News* annual statistical issues, *Automotive Industries*, *Thunderbird Scoop* by Vintage Thunderbird Club International, and *Big Bird* by Thunderbird Owners of America.

1972
All models 57,815
Total **57,814**
No separate records were kept for A-equipped 460-ci engine or sunroof-equipped T-Birds.
w/ bucket seats 8,036
w/ bench seat 49,778
w/ vinyl roof 56,831
w/ painted roof 983

1973
All Models 87,269
Total **87,269**
No separate records were kept for A-equipped 460-ci engine or sunroof-equipped T-Birds.
w/ vinyl roof 86,614
w/ painted roof 655

1974
All Models 58,443
Total **58,443**
No separate records were kept for optional models or for sun/moonroof-equipped T-Birds.

1975
All Models 42,685
Total **42,685**
No separate records were kept for optional models or for sun/moonroof-equipped T-Birds.

1976
All Models 52,935
Total **52,935**
No separate records were kept for optional models or for sun/moonroof-equipped T-Birds.
1972–1976 Sources: *Automotive News* annual statistical issues and *Chilton's Automotive Industries*.

1977
302-ci V-8 318,140
Total **318,140**
*No separate records were kept for base coupe or Town Landau models or engines.
w/ bucket seats 27,360
w/ bench seats 290,780
w/ vinyl roof 285,053
*No separate records were kept for sun/moonroofs.

1978
Base Coupe, Town Landau 333,757
Diamond Jubilee Edition 18,994
Total **352,751**
*No separate records were kept for base coupe or Town Landau models.
302-ci V-8 352,751
*No separate records were kept for base coupe or Town Landau models or engines.
w/ bucket seats 22,223
w/ bench seats 330,528
w/ vinyl roof 295,958
w/ T-roof convertible 15,168
*No separate records were kept for sun/moonroofs.

1979
302-ci V-8 284,141
Total **284,141**
*No separate records were kept for base coupe, Town Landau, or Heritage models or engines.
w/ bucket seats 12,047
w/ bench seats 272,094
w vinyl roof 215,947
w/ sunroof/moonroof 10,513
w/ T-roof convertible 12,218

1980
200-ci I-6 6,115
255-ci V-8 150,688
Total **156,803**
No separate records were kept for base coupe, Town Landau, or Silver Anniversary models or V-8 engines.
w/ bucket seats 7,056
w/ bench seats 149,747
w/ vinyl roof 127,638
w/ pop-up sunroof 9,722

1981
200-ci I-6 14,218
255-ci V-8 72,475
Total 86,693
No separate records were kept for base coupe, Town Landau, or Heritage models or V-8 engines.
w/ bucket seats 2,948
w/ bench seats 272,094
w/ vinyl roof 39,359
w/ pop-up sunroof 4,595

1982
200-ci I-6 2,618
3.8L V-6 14,807
255-ci V-8 27,717
Total **45,142**
No separate records were kept for base coupe, Town Landau, or Heritage models or V-8 engines.
w/ bucket seats 858
w/ bench seats 44,284
w/ vinyl roof 40,402
w/ pop-up sunroof 3,295
1977–1982 Sources: *Automotive News* annual statistical issues and *Chilton's Automotive Industries*.

1983
3.8L 70,515
5.0L 39,918
2.4L Turbo Coupe five-speed
   manual transmission 12,566
Total **121,999**
No separate records were kept for base coupe and Heritage models.
w/ pop-up sunroof 2,684

1984
3.8L 98,749
5.0L 56,282
2.4L Turbo Coupe automatic overdrive ... 3,093
2.4L Turbo Coupe five-speed manual transmission 11,427
Total **170,551**
No separate records were kept for base coupe, FILA, and 'Elan models.
w/ pop-up sunroof 14,838

1985
3.8L 78,963
5.0L 47,085
5.0L 30th Anniversary Edition 5,000
2.4L Turbo Coupe automatic overdrive ...8,808
2.4L Turbo Coupe five-speed
manual transmission 12,148
Total **151,852**
No separate records were kept for base coupe, FILA, and 'Elan models.
w/ pop-up sunroof 11,541

1986
3.8L 112,525
5.0L 31,865
2.4L Turbo Coupe automatic overdrive ...8,172
2.4L Turbo Coupe five-speed
manual transmission 13,403
Total **165,965**
No separate records were kept for base coupe and 'Elan models.
w/ moonroof 11,601

1987
3.8L 75,860
5.0L 28,463
2.4L Turbo Coupe automatic overdrive ...7,487
2.4L Turbo Coupe five-speed
manual transmission 15,325
Total **128,135**
No separate records were kept for base coupe, Sport, and LX models.
w/ moonroof 8,009

1988
3.8L 68,174
5.0L 41,817
2.4L Turbo Coupe automatic overdrive ..14,557
2.4L Turbo Coupe five-speed
manual transmission 22,695
Total **147,243**
No separate records were kept for base coupe, Sport, and LX models.
w/ moonroof 18,994
1983–1988 Sources: *Automotive News* annual statistical issues and *Chilton's Automotive Industries.*

1989
3.8L 102,059
3.8L SC automatic overdrive 12,809
3.8L SC five-speed manual transmission ..8,041
Total 122,909
No separate records were kept for base coupe and LX models.
w/ moonroof 17,230

1990
3.8L 82,636
3.8L SC automatic overdrive 21,966
3.8L SC five-speed manual transmission ..6,067
3.8L SC 35th Anniversary edition 3,371
Total 114,040
No separate records were kept for base coupe and LX models.
w/ moonroof 20,502

1991
3.8L 59,543
5.0L 16,232
3.8L SC automatic overdrive 7,039
3.8L SC five-speed manual transmission ..1,905
Total **84,719**
No separate records were kept for base coupe and LX models.
w/ moonroof 10,103

1992
3.8L 57,119
5.0L 12,562
3.8L SC automatic overdrive 4,212
3.8L SC five-speed manual transmission ..1,256
Total **75,149**
No separate records were kept for base coupe and LX models.
w/ moonroof 9,015

1993
3.8L LX 106,234
5.0L LX 19,587
3.8L SC automatic overdrive 3,891
3.8L SC five-speed manual transmission ..1,038
Total **130,750**

1994
4.6L LX 66,657
3.8L LX 51,056
3.8L SC automatic overdrive 2,647
3.8L SC five-speed manual transmission 722
Total **121,082**

1995
4.6L LX 94,155
3.8L LX 14,927
3.8L SC automatic overdrive 5,741
3.8L SC 5-speed manual transmission 574
Total **115,397**

1996
4.6L LX 86,522
3.8L LX 25,780
Total **112,302**

1997
4.6L LX 66,320
3.8L LX 18,956
Total **85,276**
1989–1997 Sources: *Automotive News* Annual Statistical Issues and *Chilton's Automotive Industries.*

2002
Deluxe w/ soft top only 280
Deluxe w/ hardtop 1,686
Premium w/ soft top only 2,785
Premium w/ hardtop 26,170
Neiman Marcus Edition 200
Total **31,121**

2003
Deluxe w/ soft top only 700
Deluxe w/ hardtop 691
Premium w/ soft top only 847
Premium w/ hardtop 11,574
007 Edition 694*
Total **14,506**
*694 "007" cars were sold, and an additional 6 were used for promotional and display purposes.
2002–2003 Sources: Ford Motor Company and *Porthole Authority* website.

There are no production figures available for years 2004 to 2006

Index

1955 Thunderbird, 22
1957 Thunderbird, 30
1957 Skyliner, 81
1961 Thunderbird, 53, 54, 56
1962 Thunderbird, 63
1963 1/2 Limited Edition Monaco Landau, 60
1963 Thunderbird, 69
1965 Special Landau, 74, 75
1967 Thunderbird, 91
1969 Boss 302, 99
1969 Thunderbird, 95
1975 Copper Edition, 107
1976 Thunderbird, 114
1977 Thunderbird, 122
1978 Thunderbird, 117, 120
1980 Silver Anniversary Edition, 128
1980 Thunderbird, 129
1984 FILA Edition, 137
1985 FILA Edition, 138
1988 Medium Red Clearcoat Metallic Turbo Coupe, 152
1989 Cougar XR-7, 156
1992 Thunderbird, 160
1997 Thunderbird, 170
2002 Thunderbird, 175
Accessories, 43
   Air conditioner, 46, 54, 72, 81, 90, 91, 182, 111–113, 122, 141
   Automatic climate control, 93
   Cruise control, 86, 89
   Cruise-O-Matic transmission, 43, 44, 49, 53, 59, 81
   Color TV, 87
   Keyless entry system, 131
   Mobile telephone, 87
   Radio, 54, 64, 72, 89
   Power sunroof, 49, 87, 91, 95, 102, 105
   Seatbelts, 101, 122
American Graffiti, 24
American Motors Corporation, 44
American Specialty Company, 49
Arkus-Duntov, Zora, 157
Automatic transmission, 49, 143
Automotive Manufacturers Association, 31
Beauchamp, Johnny, 47
Bordinat, Gene, 102, 129
Boyer, Bill, 84, 129, 145
Brakes, 43, 49
   Antilock brakes, 150
   Disc brakes, 92
   Drum brakes, 56

Budd Corporation, 19, 49
Buick Riviera, 78, 86, 103, 107, 111
Cadillac El Dorado, 107
Caldwell, Phillip, 129
Case, Tom, 53
Centennial Edition Thunderbird, 185
Chevrolet Monte Carlo, 98, 107, 118, 144, 151
Chicago Assembly Plant, 132
Chrysler Cordoba, 118
Chrysler LeBaron, 151
Color options, 20, 27, 29–33, 43, 46, 54, 58, 62–64, 71, 72, 75, 77, 89, 95, 106, 109, 113, 115, 117, 121, 124, 125, 129–132, 137, 144, 164, 165, 167, 168, 176, 181, 182, 184, 186, 187
Daytona 500, 47
Daytona Speed Week, 29
Dearborn Assembly, 18, 35, 162, 175
Detroit Auto Show, 17, 180, 187
Emblems, 23, 27, 34, 43, 44, 58, 64, 67, 70, 75, 77, 92, 95, 97, 112, 109, 141, 149, 155, 164, 165, 167, 173
Engine options, 22, 43, 49, 57, 59, 63, 65, 68, 98, 110, 118, 125, 131, 163
Exterior, 19, 43, 47, 55, 111, 115, 148, 165, 184, 187
   Fenders, 30, 32, 37, 39, 43, 44, 51, 54, 64, 71, 78, 86, 89, 91, 129, 155, 164, 184
   Frames, 39, 64
   Grille, 42, 47, 54, 58, 69, 73, 75, 79, 84, 90, 92, 94, 99, 101, 105, 107, 112, 125, 144, 149, 180
   Headlights, 37, 46, 84, 85, 99, 101, 107, 112, 164
   Taillight, 42, 43, 47, 55, 68, 71, 75, 78, 81, 88, 92, 94, 97, 112, 120, 161
Ford, Bill, 183
Ford, Henry, II, 11, 25, 98, 53, 102, 129
Ford, William Clay, Jr. 180
France, Bill, 47
Gaffka, Doug, 177
General Motors, 15, 110, 98
Geneva International Auto Show, 180
Heritage edition, 119, 123, 137, 139, 141
Iacocca, Lido A. "Lee", 59, 84, 102, 129, 177
Indianapolis 500, 56
Indianapolis Motor Speedway, 56
Interior, 19, 23, 30, 41, 46, 47, 55, 56, 61, 75, 77, 88, 92, 101, 105, 115, 124, 141, 142, 153, 159, 165, 167, 184, 187

Dashboard, 30, 54, 103, 109, 123, 137, 143, 159, 164, 167
James Bond films, 184
Kelly, Grace, 64
Kisler, Rich, 174
Knudsen, Sermon E. "Bunkie", 92, 97, 98, 107, 101–103, 177
Limited Edition "Princess Grace", 64
Limited Edition Landaus, 60
Lincoln Continental Mark II, 53
Lincoln Continental Mark III, 94, 107
Lincoln Continental Mark IV, 107, 110, 111
Lincoln Continental Mark VII, 136
Lincoln Continental Mark VIII, 163, 169, 174
Lincoln Continental Mark X, 187
Lincoln Town Car, 179
Martin, Mark, 168-171
Mays, J. 177
McNamara, Robert S., 23, 24, 29, 33, 39, 44, 47, 53, 56, 69, 177
Monaco Landau, 58, 59, 63, 65, 68, 69, 72, 75, 77, 83, 89, 91, 92, 94, 95, 97, 101, 122
Motor Trend, 44, 78, 151, 183
Najjar, John, 74
Nasser, Jacques "Jac", 175, 177, 183
Oldsmobile Starfire, 58, 65
Oldsmobile Toronado, 80, 107
Organization of Petroleum Exporting Countries (OPEC), 113, 118
Ornes, Allen, 158
Oros, Joe, 53
Pacific Coast Roadster, 187
Palomino show car, 74, 78
Peterson, Bob, 111
Peterson, Donald, 53
Petty, Lee, 47
Pico Rivera plant, 95, 111, 114, 118
Plymouth Sundance, 151
Pontiac Bonneville, 151
Pontiac Grand Prix, 58, 65, 92, 107, 136
Production, 19, 23, 33, 54, 186
Querfeld, Art, 71
Roush, Jack, 169
Seating choices, 46
  Bench seat, 100, 150
  Bucket seats, 86, 88, 95, 101, 102, 109, 113, 121
  Leather seats, 89, 113
  Split bench, 109, 113, 122
  Vinyl seats, 89, 121
Shinoda, Larry, 98, 99, 107
Silver Anniversary Edition, 127, 130-131
Sommers, Suzanne, 24
Sports Roadster, 57, 58, 64, 65, 74
Street-legal installations, 33, 46

Studebaker Golden Hawks, 31
Studebaker Gran Turismo Hawk, 58
Styling, 58, 64, 68
Super Coupe, 155, 159-160, 162-163, 165, 167
Telnack, Jack, 174, 177
Top options, 23, 40, 54, 71, 64
  Automatic top, 46
  Blind-quarter roof, 95, 97
  Carriage roof, 132
  Convertible, 43, 51, 53, 54, 56, 58, 59, 63, 64, 120, 124, 178, 187
  Hard top, 23, 25, 27, 29, 31, 41, 49, 52, 56, 58, 62, 63, 68, 71, 72, 77, 78, 81, 84, 90, 91, 95, 101, 103, 181–185, 187
Porthole top, 25, 27
Removable hardtop, 182
Soft top, 23, 27, 187
Sports roof hardtop, 101, 109
  Vinyl roof, 77, 91, 92, 102, 106, 111, 124, 125
Town Landau, 78, 79, 121, 124, 131–133
Transmission, 23, 56
Troutman, Alex, 180
Turbo Coupe, 137, 135, 139-144, 152, 153, 156, 158, 160
Turner, Dave, 158, 174
Walker, George, 18, 53
Warneke, Don, 174
Watts, George, 111, 169
Windows, 112
  B-pillar windows, 117, 121, 125, 131, 129, 130, 141
  C-pillar windows, 117
  Opera windows, 113
  Power windows, 56, 77, 109, 113, 122, 137, 141, 182
Wixom Assembly Plant, 47, 49, 63, 91, 95, 114, 118, 175, 178, 181, 185
World War II, 9, 11, 118